Ready, Set, Thrive - Essential Life Skills for Teens

The Ultimate Teenage Roadmap to Thriving in Today's Dynamic World

S Connor

Table of Contents

Introduction

"The quality of your life is built on the quality of your decisions."

– Wesam Fawzi

Did you know that by the time you finish reading this sentence, someone, somewhere in the world, will have made a decision that could potentially change their life forever? Life is full of moments like these, choices both big and small—that shape who we are and who we become. Welcome to the journey of mastering life skills, where every decision counts, and every skill learned opens doors to endless possibilities.

Are you thrilled to begin the next chapter of your life? Or are you just sitting there thinking, what's next? That's fine! Walking into the teenage phase feels like being handed a Rubik's cube; every side is a different mess. You go through this whole identity shift, which makes you feel out of place and often misunderstood. You have all this energy, talent, skills, and mindset to move mountains. Yet, you feel so emotionally confounded and mentally distracted, with no clue. Without learning basic life skills, whether it's cooking, smart buying, budgeting, money management, communication skills, goal or time setting, going through this transition seems like stepping into a blindfolded battlefield. You never know what will hit you at the next step! Whereas, with essential life skills such as your tools and armor, you can take every challenge head-on and preempt every single move before life lands you into trouble. You simply take charge of your future.

"But wait! Am I not learning all that in school?" If that has crossed your mind, you are not alone. Yes! Your school plays a huge role in shaping your personality. It is a place where you learn the causes of World War II, how to compute the area of a square, or the intricacies of The Great Gatsby. Still, those everyday life skills are rarely taught in the classrooms. You can learn to do the math, but how to use it to handle your money and invest are some things you won't find in your school curriculum.

Don't worry! **"Ready, Set, Thrive - Essential Life Skills for Teens"** is here to guide you. This book will be your secret companion to which you can reach out whenever you face trouble managing your time, money, or relationships. I know there is immense peer pressure and competition out there, where you feel like a walking failure, and as if everyone around you has it all figured out, but that's not true! Those problems you are facing right now certainly do not define who you are. Starting today, you can turn the narrative of your own story by practicing all the life skills we are about to explore in this guide. From study methods to time management and organization skills, this book brings you closer to some of the most effective techniques, like Pomodoro and Eisenhower Matrix. These sections are not just stuffed with words and fluff - there are some fascinating timetables, and study planner ideas that are crafted to help you visualize your daily schedule and stick to it.

Communication is another significant challenge that I see most teens dealing with these days. One day, you are a carefree child, then the teenage hits you, and suddenly, you are a grown-up who is expected to talk and behave in a particular manner. This new level of expectation and changing life roles leads to communication anxiety and a perpetual fear of misunderstanding. But you know what? As John Powell said, **"Communication works for those who work at it."** You can learn to be a pro-negotiator or an excellent speaker with a little effort. So set your worries aside if you ever feel ashamed or embarrassed to speak your mind, as this guidebook brings you some of the most effective techniques to sharpen your communication skills and boost your confidence. That's not it! There are tons of strategies that will help you enhance your decision-making and leadership skills. Using those methods, you can not only boost your self-esteem but also develop emotional resilience to get through life's ebb and flow.

Our journey will not stop there! Are you having trouble saving those extra bucks or struggling to figure out how to keep your credit scores high? Or how to avoid the student debt trap? Don't fret! The chapter on money management skills has various exciting ideas and strategies to make you pocket-smart! Then, the chapters that follow will help you become digitally literate, more conscious, and well-groomed. Lastly, there is a bonus chapter at the end that will give you some great tips to empower yourself and learn the art of becoming a confident individual who takes charge and leads others in various spheres of life. Trust me! After giving this book a good read, you will emerge as a more confident and stronger individual, capable of making real changes in life.

"Who am I to advise you on how to spend your teenage years?" Well, after having spent several years powering through the intricacies of the corporate world, I have come to understand the importance of equipping every young mind with the tools they need to thrive in this ever-evolving professional landscape. When I reflect on my own teenage years, I realize that I was really fortunate to have a supportive family environment. My upbringing offered me a solid foundation upon which I could build my life. Today, as a mother of two incredible children, I draw upon my experiences to guide them through their own journeys. My eldest child has already stepped into the exciting journey of young adulthood, while my younger one is on the cusp of venturing into the tumultuous yet transformative teenage years. So, I have first-hand experience witnessing the challenges of being a teenager in this era.

I approach this book as an author through this lens of personal experience and professional insight. As a lifelong learner, I constantly search for new knowledge and insights to share with you. Through the content of this book, I want to bridge the gap between the classroom and real-world success. From effective communication to decision-making and emotional intelligence, my goal is to equip you with the essential skills you need to succeed in all facets of life. Through engaging anecdotes, actionable advice, and proven strategies, I strive to create a resource that not only informs but also inspires you to embrace your potential and confidently chart your course toward a fulfilling future. But more than just practical advice, I am here to offer guidance, empathy, and a healthy dose of encouragement as you embark on this new journey of self-discovery.

The road ahead is indeed full of bumps and challenges, so every time you stumble, remember to be kind to yourself and those around you. You can truly discover your inner potential and channel it in the right direction with kindness and empathy.

So, are you all set and ready to begin? Let's dive straight in and explore the essential life skills that will set you up for success during your teenage years and beyond. These skills will enhance your academic performance and empower you to navigate life's challenges confidently and easily. From effective communication and time management to problem-solving and financial literacy, these skills will help you establish a strong foundation for a successful and fulfilling life. Get ready to start this exciting journey of personal growth and discovery!

CHAPTER 1

The Essential Life Skills for Adolescent Success

How can one achieve success in life? Is there a foolproof formula to unlock the secrets of a fulfilling and successful life? Frankly, there isn't one! As we grow up, we each paint different pictures of our future selves— some aspire to be doctors, engineers, or architects, while others dream of careers in acting, entrepreneurship, art, or music. While professional achievements are often seen as a measure of life's success, they are not the sole determinants.

True fulfillment comes from various facets, like financial stability, healthy relationships, mental wellness, spiritual resilience, and harmonious family life. While schools and colleges focus on preparing us for the professional front, they often overlook teaching essential life skills like time management, organization, communication, and emotional intelligence. Without these skills, navigating the challenges of adulthood can feel like an uphill battle. Let's delve deeper and explore the significance and impact of each life skill to understand how they can guide us toward our ultimate life aspirations and ideals.

The Value of Life Skills

"Life skills" - They are not just some boring stuff that adults go on about. Consider them your secret weapon for life's long quest. If you have ever been into gaming, like Fortnite or anything similar, then you will totally get what I am saying here. Life is a bit like those games. You are constantly facing different challenges, just like picking weapons in the game. But instead of guns and stuff, your weapons are life skills.

Let's say you are forced to make the tough decision of picking majors for college; now, skills like smart decision-making can help you in this regard. Or when you are working on a group project with your classmates, that's when communication and conflict resolution skills become your superpowers. Each life skill we will discuss at length here is super important. Together, they make you a total ninja, just like your favorite game character, ready to take on anything life throws your way.

Relationship Building

Can you imagine yourself without your family, friends, and loved ones? How would you feel? Terrible? Of course! We all are social beings who crave emotional connections. Having meaningful bonds in life gives us a sense of purpose and helps us climb that success ladder quickly. Healthy relationships are some of the most prized possessions that we often don't realize. Whether it's the professional realm or personal affairs, we must strengthen existing connections and constantly build new ones to steer ahead in life. This is where mastering the following skills can help! From strengthening your bond with parents to resolving conflicts with siblings or managing teamwork with friends and classmates, these skills will help you take charge of every conversation or interaction you have with those around you.

- **Communication:**

"Communication is the solvent of all problems and is the foundation for personal development."

- Peter Shepherd

When you step into the teenage, you go through this whole identity shift where you experience all sorts of physical, cognitive, and emotional changes, which often lead to mood swings, heightened sensitivity, and difficulty expressing yourselves effectively. You feel like nobody gets you! But that's not true. It simply means you need effective communication skills to let the world understand you. Being able to express yourself clearly and really listen helps you connect on a whole other level. Plus, when you have solid communication skills, you are not afraid to speak up for yourself and set those all-important boundaries.

Think about it! You are better at saying what you need, standing up to peer pressure, and making sure your voice is heard. And let's not forget about school! Nailing communication also means acing group projects, nailing presentations, and getting your ideas across loud and clear. When things get tough, those communication skills come in handy for resolving conflicts like a boss, keeping the drama to a minimum, and keeping the vibes positive. So yes! Mastering communication is not just about talking; it is about owning your space, rocking your relationships, and crushing it in every aspect of your life.

- **Taking Up Responsibility**

Now, you must be wondering what responsibility has to do with creating good connections. Well, when you learn to take responsibility for your actions, decisions, and even your mistakes, you are basically telling the world, "I have got this." You own up to your stuff, whether it is acing your school test or admitting when you have messed up. By doing so, you gain great respect from others. People see you as a reliable, trustworthy, and mature person, leaving a lasting impression. Most importantly, when you know you can handle your business, you feel highly confident and ready to take on whatever life throws your way.

- **Empathy**

Being empathetic simply means standing in other people's shoes and understanding their actions and reactions. Understanding others is often difficult when you see things only from your perspective. Still, when you step into their role and genuinely understand their origin, you react accordingly. Empathy makes you a better team player; it creates an atmosphere of support and creativity everywhere. Moreover, when you learn to be empathetic towards others, you also learn to be kind to yourself, which is essential when dealing with the harsh challenges of teenage and young adulthood. So, by learning to be empathetic, you build strong bonds with others and yourself.

- **Conflict Resolution**

Let's face it! Disagreements are inevitable. Big or small conflicts are bound to happen with family members, friends, loved ones, or acquaintances. And you see! Having conflicts with someone isn't bad; they can help you create even better and stronger bonds with people if you successfully put effective conflict-resolution skills to use. They are the sidekicks that help you work through disagreements and find solutions everyone can agree on. From sibling squabble to a bigger family issue, when you know how to handle conflicts calmly and respectfully, you keep the peace and strengthen your relationships.

Practical Life Skills

Soon, you will leave your nest and enter the real world, where every day will be a new struggle. Whether living in college dorms or setting up your own living space, there are some practical skills, such as cooking your own meals, cleaning up, doing laundry, managing expenses, budgeting, and personal care, which will be your life savior. With these skills, you can confidently deal with life's day-to-day challenges. Some practical skills that every growing individual must learn include:

- **Household Skills**

From doing your own laundry to cooking a simple meal, cleaning up after yourself, and fixing a leaky faucet, these are some basic tasks that every young adult must learn to become fully independent. They might not seem glamorous, but knowing how to carry them out will make your life much easier. Whether living with roommates in college or on your own, with these skills in hand, you will never have to reach out to others for help.

- **Financial Skills**

If you learn to take care of your finances now, you will never have to worry about money matters in the future. Financial knowledge and skills are more than just simple math; they are more about developing a strong sense of smart budgeting, saving extra bucks for rainy days, avoiding debt traps, investing in your education, and avoiding impulse buying. You might not earn much right now, but how you manage those allowances and spend them today will significantly shape your financial standing tomorrow.

- **Self-Care**

As teens, life is pretty hectic and tough, right? Between school, extracurriculars, and maybe even a part-time job, it can feel like juggling a million things simultaneously. But trust me! Burning out is no joke. That is why putting your health first is crucial, creating realistic schedules, and making self-care a regular part of your routine. Nowadays, with everything so competitive, it is easy to get caught up in the race to success and forget about your well-being. But here is the deal! None of your achievements will matter if you are unhealthy enough to enjoy them. That is why self-care is a crucial skill you need to take seriously. When you put self-care first, you are not just thinking about the here and now! You are investing in your future happiness and health. You owe it to yourself to stay happy, healthy, and excelling at everything you do!

Executive Functioning Skills

Take these skills as cognitive abilities that help you control, organize, and regulate your thoughts, actions, and behaviors. See! Our thoughts and ideas are not just floating around aimlessly – they shape our actions and behaviors. By mastering how to wrangle those thoughts, you lay down the blueprint for how you want to move through the world. These skills, which we call executive functioning skills, are like your personal life coaches. They are the ones who help you adapt to new situations, plan out your next move, and tackle challenges like a boss. And here is the coolest part, they are not just handy for school stuff. Nope, they are helpful in almost every area of your life, from that math test to navigating friendships and even figuring out who you want to be when you grow up. Let me explain how!

- **Smart Planning**

With smart planning, you become the captain of your own ship. You have your eyes set on a treasure - your goals and charting your course to get there. It is simply about knowing where you want to go and determining the best route. Whether saving up for that new game you have had your eye on or studying for that big upcoming test, having a solid plan is key. Life is full of distractions and curveballs, but you can steer through the choppy waters and stay on course with a clear map or plan.

- **Staying Organized**

Let's imagine that you open your cupboard, and voila! Your clothes are neatly folded and sorted by color – whites on one side and colors on the other. Easy peasy! Right? You can grab what you need in a flash. But hold up! What if that same cupboard was a chaotic mess? Clothes all jumbled up, nowhere to be found. No less than a nightmare! That is where organization skills come in clutch. They are your secret weapon for keeping your life in order. Good organization skills are your superheroes that keep everything sorted, whether your books on the shelf, your room, your studies, or your day-to-day activities. They help you quickly tackle everything, keeping things balanced and running smoothly. So, next time you feel overwhelmed, remember - a little organization goes a long way!

- **Time Management**

Time is both a foe and a friend. When taken seriously and utilized smartly, time can be our biggest ally. But when you are slacking off or letting the minutes slip away, it feels like time has the upper hand, and you are left scrambling to catch up. That is why mastering time management is really important. Effective time management is about making every minute count, whether crushing that homework assignment, hanging out with friends, or enjoying your favorite hobbies. With excellent time management skills, you are getting things done and owning your day like a boss. So, next time you feel like there is never enough time, remember that you can make every minute count. Use it wisely, and watch how it transforms your world!

- **Task Management**

Taking care of your everyday "to-do list" is what task management is mainly about. You know those big, scary tasks that seem impossible to conquer? Guess what? When you break tasks down into bite-sized chunks, suddenly, they are not so daunting. You take one step at a time, as Lao Tzu said in the Tao Te Ching, "***The journey of a thousand miles begins with a single step***." And it is true! Whether studying for an exam, cleaning up your room, or working on a passion project, task management is your ticket to success.

- **Emotional Regulation**

Think of your emotions like the weather forecast-they are constantly changing, sometimes sunny, sometimes stormy. One moment, you are on cloud nine; the next, you feel like a thundercloud. It is all part of being human. But the thing is that when you let your emotions run wild, you step out into a hurricane without an umbrella. You end up making impulsive decisions that you might regret later. Not cool, right? That is where emotional regulation comes into play. Emotional regulation is your own personal umbrella. It helps you weather the storm of your feelings, understand what is happening inside, and find healthy ways to deal with it. So, whether you are riding high on happiness or drowning in a sea of sadness, always remember that the power to calm the storm and find your way back to sunny skies lies inside you!

Critical Thinking Skills

Today, we all live in a post-truth era, where, every day, hundreds of gigabits of information are shared over the internet, and not all of it is true. Without critical thinking skills, we can easily fall prey to unnecessary propaganda and misinformation. When you critically assess every piece of information that meets your eye, evaluate the credibility of its source, analyze it from different perspectives, and then develop an opinion based on merits, facts, and evidence - you discover the reality of the situation and act accordingly. This approach broadens your mindset and keeps your mind open to new possibilities. Here is what happens when you learn to think critically!

- **You Solve Problems Like a Boss**

Let's say you have a school test tomorrow, and there is this really tough math problem you cannot seem to crack. The clock is ticking, and tension is rising. What would you do in such a scenario? Will you start searching for online resources and textbooks or call your friends to discuss possible solutions? If so, then your problem-solving game is right on point! Our mindset and efforts to solve problems in difficult situations are essential tools we fail to realize. Without this skill, people give up before even trying. Effective problem-solving makes you resilient against all the hardships of life, and you battle against all the odds like a leader.

- **You Make Smart Decisions**

"Should I buy a new pair of your favorite sneakers? Or do I have to save that money for my upcoming school project?" Which majors should I choose for college?" I get it! It is never easy to make decisions as tough as these. There is always something at stake when you pick between the two attractive options. Now, there are two ways to reach a decision. The first is to listen to your heart, act impulsively, and forget about the ultimate consequences. This approach may give you instant gratification, but it is loaded with risk and is definitely not beneficial in the long run. The other one is to consider all the options, weigh their pros and cons, consider your long-term goals, and choose the one that best aligns with your priorities. And that, my friend! We call informed decision-making. This skill minimizes the risks and increases the likelihood of positive outcomes.

- **You Stand Up for What Is Right**

Critical thinking skills give you the courage and intelligence to stand up for yourself and those who cannot speak for themselves. It is about being brave enough to fight for what is right, even when it feels like an uphill battle. When you have that courage, you become a force to be reckoned with, a voice for change in a world that sometimes needs a little shaking up. And even when it feels like you are standing alone, you are never truly alone. There are always people who will believe in you and your cause, and together, you can make a real difference.

- **Respect the Differences**

Having disagreements is totally normal; it is a natural part of life. But it is also a sign that you are speaking your mind, which is super cool. Critical thinking is your guide through those disagreements. It teaches you to be open-minded, listen to what others say, and speak up for your beliefs without throwing shade at anyone else. It gives you the confidence to stand firm in your beliefs and stay humble enough to learn from others. See, the thing is, when you approach disagreements with this mindset, you no longer see yourself winning or losing. You seek them from the perspective of growth and understanding.

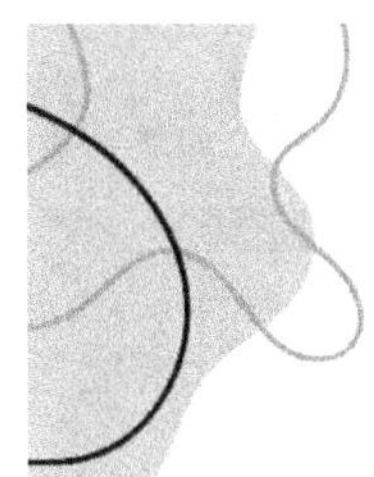

THE THOUGHT TREK

Are you wondering if you already have the power of critical thinking, or do you need to polish your skills to begin making better decisions in life and solve all your problems with a positive mindset? Then stop for a minute! This quick "thought trek" activity brings you some powerful brain teasing prompts and questions to self-reflect and assess your critical thinking capabilities. Don't worry! It's not a quiz, it is just a little introspection session where you will find the answers that lie within you. Sit back, relax, and simply give these prompts some thought to analyze your thinking and behavior patterns.

- Let's say you just came across a meme claiming a famous singer left school to pursue music. It seems wild, right? How would you check if it is true or just gossip?

____

____

- While looking for the truth about the singer, which reliable sources of information would you use? Official websites, news bits, or interviews?

____

____

- Movie night's coming up, and your crew is split between scary flicks and comedies. How would you pick something everyone likes?

____

____

- You are having a group project discussion, and you disagree with the idea of a teammate. How would you voice your opinion respectfully while listening to their perspective?

____

____

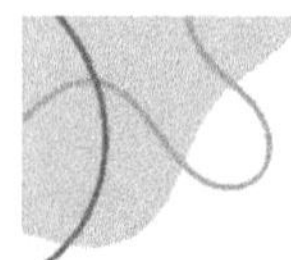

THE
THOUGHT
TREK

- Imagine you are working on a science fair project with your friend. Now your pal hasn't finished their share of work, and the presentation is the next day! How would you approach your partner about this without creating conflict?

____

____

- In the above given scenario, would you like to help your partner catch up? What would you do? And how would you delegate the rest of the work to nail that presentation?

____

____

- Reflect on your decision-making process when faced with peer pressure or difficult choices. How do you stay true to your values and beliefs while also considering the perspectives of others?

____

____

- You spot someone getting bullied online. Would you stand up for them? Do you think jumping in directly is safe? If not, who can you tell?

____

____

- Do you want to improve your math grades? What would be your action plan?

____

____

- Would you set up a study plan for the tough stuff, meet your classmates for a study group, or find some tutor? And how would you check if your plan is working?

____

____

- Picture yourself in a VR game 20 years down the line. What new technological advancements could you see?

____

____

If you didn't get the answers to all the above questions straightaway, then don't worry! Self-reflection is a long, complex process that takes both time and patience. This quick questionnaire will provoke your thoughts and help you unearth your critical thinking capabilities. If you love to question everything around you, rely more on facts and less on opinion, and respect everyone's point of view while standing firm by your own knowledge then, you, my friend, are definitely a critical thinker. However, it is not a one-time thing; the process of becoming a critical thinker never stops. There is always room for improvement, and that is where the upcoming chapters of this book will guide you.

Now that you have reached the end of the first chapter of your teenage guide, congratulations! You are doing great! Just keep going. In this chapter, I highlighted the importance and role of some essential life skills that every person should learn to climb the ladder of success on both professional and personal fronts. The life skills that remained the basis of this chapter included effective communication, organizational and managerial skills, household and financial skills, and critical thinking.

It is true that learning these skills is an endeavor full of struggles and challenges, but don't worry! I am here to guide you at every step of the way. We will look deeply into each skill, its various aspects, and the effective strategies and techniques you will find in the coming chapters. Your journey to socially, emotionally, and intellectually prosper in all spheres of life is about to begin. During this process, stay kind to yourself, keep your mind open to new possibilities, and don't hesitate to ask for help from your parents, teachers, school counselors, siblings, and friends. They are often the ones dearest to you and become your strongest support, so reach out and share your problems and struggles to find constructive solutions.

CHAPTER 2

Effective Study Methods & Essential Techniques

"Education is the passport to the future, for tomorrow belongs to those who prepare for it today."

— **Malcolm X**

The lifelong process of learning never stops! Today, you are in school and will soon step into a college or a university. And I get it! Studying often feels like trying to juggle a dozen balls at once. With so many subjects, assignments, and distractions vying for your attention, it is no wonder concentration can feel like a distant dream. But don't worry! There are various effective study methods and techniques that you can keep in your life skills toolbox and use every time you face difficulty managing time, learning a concept, or preparing for a test. From breaking down huge tasks into smaller chunks to creating a distraction-free study environment, there are plenty of strategies to boost your focus and productivity. So, take a deep breath, shake off the overwhelm, and let's tackle those books together. You got this!

Schedule Your Time

Studying is a race against time. You have to look through concepts, read several books, and learn to remember facts, statistics, important formulas, and whatnot, but in a limited time. Be it a test or an exam, time must be utilized effectively to prepare well for them. If you want to avoid that last-minute panic where you are sitting in your room, thinking which chapter to read or which to leave, biting your nails, and drowning in fear of failing, then you will have to learn how to schedule your time effectively.

Try Chunking

Let's say you have this big math test next week! The best technique to prepare for it is to divide the whole syllabus into chunks. If your goal is to practice and learn the whole chapter in six days, then divide this into small, manageable targets. Divide the content into 6 small parts and focus on one part each day. Or if you are assigned a task to write a 3000-word essay in 6 days, then write 500 words per day, and you will be good to go. This chunking technique can be applied to any task at hand. Just remember to stick to your set schedule and continue following the timeline.

Make an Effective Study Plan

Having a rock-solid plan keeps you focused. When you know what you are doing, it minimizes the chances of distraction, and you don't waste time contemplating what to do next. You can make a study plan for the day or the week. In this plan, mention your goals, the number of subjects to study, assignments, the timeline, and additional notes. Jake, a high school student, shared how using a planner transformed his hectic schedule. He said:

"Before, I was always forgetting assignments and deadlines. Now, I can see everything at a glance and plan my time more effectively."

Let me give you an example of a weekly study plan to help you understand what it looks like:

STUDY PLANNER

DATE

MO TU WE TH FR SA SU

STUDY HOURS

EXPECTED	HOUR	MINUTES
ACTUAL	HOUR	MINUTES

TODAYS SUBJECT

DEADLINES

STUDY PROGRESS

TIME TABLE

GOALS

NOTES & DOODLES

In this study planner, you can specify each block under each day for different subjects. For example, if you study history from 8:00 to 8:30 pm, then switch to geography from 8:30 to 9:00 pm. In this way, you can add specific tasks that need to be done on a particular day.

Distraction-Free Environment

Constant distractions are time killers! One minute, you are thinking of studying; the next, you get an Instagram notification, and before you know it, the next 30 minutes are passed by scrolling through the feed. Whether it's the constant pinging of notifications on your cellphone or someone playing games on their Play Station near you, these distractions can bind you for hours, leaving you with very little time to study effectively.

So, no matter how much time you allocate to study, be it 10 or 20 minutes, make sure to sit in a distraction-free environment. A separate study space, whether it's a corner of a room or any other secluded area in the house, is the best place to study with undivided attention. Since cell phones and their notifications can really mess with your focus, it is best to put them on silent mode and keep them away from your sight whenever you are studying. You can take breaks in between tasks to keep your mind relaxed, but never push your brain to multitask while it tries hard to learn a complex math problem or a scientific fact.

Use your study time wisely

Think of your study time as a valuable currency. You should invest it in a way that gives you the best return on investment. With so much going on in your life, from extracurricular activities to personal interests, it is crucial to be efficient with your study time to stay on top of your academic game while still enjoying other aspects of life.

- The best way to use your time effectively is to prioritize your tasks. First, identify the most important and urgent tasks, assignments, or subjects and tackle them first. Give your full attention to these tasks to make the most of your study time and get the important stuff done.

- Take frequent breaks during your study sessions. Research shows that short breaks can actually improve focus and productivity, so do not feel guilty about taking a breather every now and then.

- And whatever you do, avoid multitasking. It might seem like you are getting more done by juggling multiple tasks at once, but in reality, it just leads to lower-quality work and increased stress. Instead, focus on one task at a time and give it your full attention.

- While it may seem super tempting to study all night, especially when you have an exam tomorrow, make sure to avoid studying right before bedtime. Your brain needs time to unwind and process information, so give yourself a break before hitting the bed. During deep sleep stages, the brain consolidates and strengthens memories formed throughout the day. Information learned when you are awake is processed, organized, and stored more effectively during sleep, so give your mind the necessary sleep time to retain and recall what you have learned. Plus, a good night's sleep is vital for your physical well-being as well.

Practice For Testing

The exam time pressure is a real thing. It is one thing to learn what you will be tested for, but when you are sitting in the exam room, the clock is ticking, and you have to complete all the answers in time; that pressure can send mini panic attacks down your spine. The smart move to keep yourself calm and composed during the exam or a test is to practice beforehand for such a scenario.

Once you are done with the exam preparation and you are confident about your knowledge of the subject, set a timer and test yourself as per the similar exam room conditions. Repeat this practice before every test to assess your exam-taking skills and improve them accordingly.

Be Consistent

None of the techniques shared in this chapter will work if you aren't consistent in your efforts. If you study one day and skip the next day, then all that work will keep piling up, leaving you more stressed and panicked than before.

Remember, **"Slow and steady wins the race"**. This is exactly what you need to do. Stick to your schedule with consistency and keep it simple. In case of an emergency, if you miss out on a target, then divide the pending work across the remaining days to make up for it. Trust me! This habit of consistency is going to be your lifelong sidekick, which will not only help in your educational endeavors but in your professional life as well.

Learn the Tricks for Efficient Note-Taking

Emma, a sophomore in high school, found that rewriting her notes in her own words helped her better understand complex concepts in various subjects including Biology. By adopting this study method, she not only improved her grades but also gained a deeper understanding of the subject. This learning method wasn't limited to science This is how she shared her experience:

"When I was in high school, I struggled with memorizing historical dates until I discovered the power of mnemonic devices. I still remember acing my history exam after creating a silly story to remember all the dates and events."

How well you can prepare for a test, or a quick quiz depends on your note-making skills. If your notes are not organized and you have stuffed them with every unnecessary detail, then they will be of no use during exam preparation when you battle against time. On the flip side, well-written notes can help you revise all the concepts and help your mind memorize them quickly. To improve comprehension and remembering of important material, you just have to come up with your own system of note-taking. Here is how you can make it effective!

- First, keep your notes short and to the point. Now, I am not saying to skip important details to keep it concise, but simply summarize the whole information of a paragraph in a brief line so it would be easy to read and memorize.

- The more bullet points in your notes, the easier it gets to read through them. So, use bullet points to break the complete concept into 5-10 smaller chunks for convenient reading.

- Headings are another way to break the text into smaller sections. They make the text look more organized and easier to memorize. You can use different colors to create the headings and make them more appealing and prominent using different markers.

- ***"A picture is worth a thousand words."*** This adage commonly attributed to Fred R. Barnard, seems to be quite relatable when it comes to making notes. Adding visual aids like diagrams and charts to the notes gives them visual appeal and helps the brain to instantly pick up the concept. They not only help to understand the concept but also to memorize it. So, add diagrams and charts to your notes. For handwritten notes, you can get them printed or use those transparent (traceable) sticky notepads to trace the diagrams and stick them into your notes where needed.

- There are several online and offline applications that you can use to write notes on your computer, tablet, or laptop; these apps provide various options to add bullets, diagrams, charts, and pictures to notes. Plus, you can label the notes and categorize them according to the subject name.

- While those applications are smart ways to store large amounts of information in a limited space; and if you are comfortable using them, then that is perfect, research has shown that handwritten notes are much more effective for learning. When you write every word on paper, the brain automatically memorizes the concept to some extent. Handwritten notes are better for short and long-term memory recall as these notes are in your own words and handwriting.

Down below is a simple, organized structure for effective note-taking. You can either use this template or create your own handwritten one using a similar format.

Study Notes

Topic: _____________________

Subject: _____________________

Name: _____________________

Class: _____________________

Date: _____________________

Questions/Main Ideas

Notes

Summary

Use Creative Study Tools

Sure, conventional notes are good for learning, but when you sprinkle a little creativity over your study methods, learning becomes more fun and a lot less boring. You can best learn a concept when it sparks your imagination and helps your brain visualize the essence of it. The following methods can keep your brain from distraction and greatly help you focus.

- **Artsy Flashcards**

If you are the type of person who loves to doodle and stay creative, then flashcards can be your new best friend. As you read through your textbooks or other materials, write down key points on colorful flashcards. You can use different colors for different categories and get artistic with doodles or drawings to help retain the information in your mind. This method is especially great for visual learners who remember information better through pictures and diagrams, but it can also benefit verbal learners who learn better by writing things down.

You can create flashcards either by printing information on paper and cutting it into smaller sections or cutting a card sheet into smaller squares, then drawing an image or writing the title of the concept on one side and writing its detail on the other side of the same card. Putting all the information on cards in this way can help you learn and revise all the concepts quickly, anytime, and anywhere. Let's say you are facing difficulty memorizing the molecular structure of $NaCl$ for your chemistry test. Here is how you can create a simple flashcard to learn, memorize, and revise the concept using nothing but a card sheet.

NaCl

Sodium Chloride (Ionic Bond)

In sodium chloride (NaCl), sodium gives away an electron to chlorine. This makes sodium positive (Na^+) and chlorine negative (Cl^-). They stick together because opposite charges attract, forming a strong bond called ionic bonding.

- **Enjoy a Sing-along**

Care to make studying interesting? How about you turn your study material into catchy tunes and lyrics? Just as we learned some valuable lessons on kindness through nursery rhymes and poems, we can learn all other concepts through songs. Whether it is to learn math formulas or memorize the names of the bones in the human body, you can create your own tunes to remember this information. From Shakespeare's plots to financial concepts, turn them into musical melodies and sing away. This method is useful for auditory learners who absorb information best through hearing. Let me give you a good example of a sing-along song about human bones, their names, and their location in the body. It is a part of the song that I once watched in a Disney season, and it goes like this:

"My body's many parts

And this is where it starts

Phalanges I have ten

And metatarsals then

I got some tarsals, too

I will put them in my shoes

The fibula is next

According to my text

Then comes the tibia

That ain't no fibia

And now I'm up to my knee

Yeah, yeah, yeah

That's the patella to me"

(Miley Cirus-Bones Dance lyrics)

- **Read with Style**

Have you ever read bedtime stories to younger siblings or kids in fun character voices? You can bring that same energy to your textbook reading. While reading your study material, assign different roles to characters and concepts, read them out loud, and put on a performance like you are on stage. This can transform your dry content into engaging drama, making the material more memorable and enjoyable. You can even involve your friends by assigning them roles and making it a group activity.

- **Teach Your Friends**

They say the best way to learn is to teach, so why not become a teacher yourself? Take on the role of educator and teach someone else what you are learning. Whether it is explaining concepts to your family, friends, or even your pet, teaching others reinforces your own understanding and retention of the material. Plus, it is a fun and interactive way to study that is great for interpersonal learners.

- **Stay Active**

Who says studying has to be boring and sedentary? You can add a quick exercise regime or any physical activity to your study routine to keep both your body and mind engaged. Take a walk while listening to audiobooks from your textbooks, do push-ups or laps around the house as a reward for finishing sections, or simply stand up and stretch between study sessions. Studies show that physical activity can improve academic performance, so why not make it a part of your study routine?

Are you ready to put all those creative study techniques to the test? All it requires is a little consistency and self-discipline to keep your study sessions stress-free. The best part? All these time-tested methods are surely going to take your "study game" to the next level. They will not only help you prepare for school tests and exams, but they are equally effective for college preparation as well. From studying for your finals to memorizing concepts for your SATs or ACTs, these tools and techniques will help you a great deal.

Getting Ready for College

One of the most significant and life-altering transitions you experience during your teenage years is stepping into your college life. From the institute you select to the major you choose every little decision you make at this point is going to shape your future. Therefore, this process requires thoughtful planning, careful consideration, and implementation of an effective study regimen to earn good scores on your standardized tests. It is wise to start getting ready for college if you are already in high school or are soon getting into it.

What Does College Prep Include?

It is true that college preparation is not an easy process. But I can assure you that if you are smart about it, you can stay ahead of each step and carve your own path to get into a great institute. College preparations mainly include:

Academic Readiness: This is determined by your high school grades, CGPA, or scores on standardized tests like the SAT and ACT. Since each college or university has its own eligibility criteria to assess the academic readiness of the applicant, you have to keep your grades, CGPA, and test scores as high as required by the institutes you are aiming to join. This is where all the effective study methods and tools will help you to keep your grades up. Here is what you must try!

- **Follow a Study Schedule:** Mark the date of your SAT, ACT, or any other standardized test on your calendar, and then count the days you are left with to create a weekly or daily schedule to study according to the given time frame. In this schedule, specify a dedicated study time for each subject. Allocate time for attending classes, reviewing notes, completing assignments, and engaging in extracurricular activities as well (those are important, too!).

- **Focus on Active Learning**: Passive reading or listening to lectures does not work. It is important to use active learning techniques such as summarizing key points, teaching concepts to others, and participating in discussions or study groups to absorb all the knowledge. These methods help enhance your understanding and retention of the material.

- **Use Multiple Resources**: Never rely solely on one single textbook or lecture notes. Try to use online resources, videos, academic journals, and additional readings as well to gain different perspectives and deepen your understanding of topics.

- **Create Well-Organized Notes:** To save time, use outlines, diagrams, mind maps, and key points to create notes and memorize the concepts quickly. Regularly check your notes and organize them to focus on learning areas that need further clarification.

- **Practice All the Problems Regularly:** It is best to practice all the complex problems and exercise well before the exams and tests. Attempt online practice tests to assess your preparation and revise all the concepts.

- **Manage Your Time Smartly**: If you are preparing for the standardized test, then divide this goal into manageable targets, such as preparing for each part of the test separately. Then, set realistic deadlines for each subject.

Extracurricular Activities: Every college loves to enroll a well-rounded student who is involved in stuff outside the classroom. If your college application mentions things like being a member of drama clubs, sports teams, and volunteer groups, then that really brings a great impression to the table. Not only will it make your college application look good, but it will also help you develop leadership skills and make new friends.

Soft Skills: These are the skills that are not taught in a classroom but are super important for success in college and beyond. Things like time management, organization, communication, and critical thinking - the ones that you are learning through the text of this book, are skills that will matter the most when you step into your college life as a young adult. These skills will come in handy when you are juggling classes, assignments, and maybe even a part-time job.

College Research and Application Process: This part can feel a bit overwhelming, but don't worry – you can totally do this! Start by researching colleges that interest you and figuring out what they are looking for in applicants. Then, get familiar with the application process. Create a list of colleges against their application deadlines, essay prompts, recommendation letters, and the whole nine yards. And don't forget about financial aid – scholarships, grants, and loans – you will need to know how to navigate all that stuff, too.

Emotional and Social Preparation: College life is not just about academics; it is also about personal growth and independence. So, start working on those social skills. Make new friends, network, and learn to navigate new social situations, as it really helps build strong connections. And don't forget about taking care of yourself emotionally.

College can be stressful, so it is important to develop a healthy coping mechanism before you set foot into this new phase of life.

How to Get Parents Involved in the Process?

Your parents are your secret weapon in this whole journey. They have been around the block and know a ton about different industries and stuff. Their support, advice, and all those little nuggets of wisdom they drop are going to be super helpful for you. They have seen you grow up, so they probably have a pretty good idea of what makes you tick. Talking with them about your dreams and goals is a great move. Share what is on your mind, ask questions, and let them know what you are curious about when it comes to prepping for college. Even if you don't always see eye-to-eye, it is still worth hearing them out. Every bit of advice they give can help you make smarter choices for your future. So, don't hesitate to lean on them for support and soak up all that parental wisdom!

Always keep in mind that you are talented and capable of doing what you set out for! You just need a little self-belief and smart planning to achieve your ultimate goals. Whenever I am asked about good career advice, I always think of this beautiful quote by Paulo Coelho that encapsulates the very essence of the discussion we had in this chapter.

"Whatever you decide to do, make sure it makes you happy."

The journey between high school and college is indeed an uphill battle, but if you successfully steer through those struggles and challenges, you will turn out to be a stronger and more confident adult. Stay open to new experiences, travel more often, connect with progressive people, and create a network of your own to learn about all the rising opportunities. In this age and time, the more dynamic you become, the easier it gets to climb the success ladder. Just keep going and also support others along the way.

With that being said, we have concluded another chapter of this book. And just like that, you have mastered the art of studying with fewer distractions and more focus. Managing studies with other routine activities is indeed difficult. Add the fear of shaping a great career to the equation, and you feel like you are constantly carrying this heavy weight on your shoulders. However, by employing the techniques and strategies shared in this chapter, such as prioritizing assignments, breaking down work, creating realistic goals, and organizing your stuff, you can definitely get rid of that unnecessary burden and make studies a little less boring and a lot more fun. There is yet another skill set that will help you organize your life and manage your studies with all other activities of your choice like a pro, and that is "time management and organization." In the next chapter, we are about to explore some of the most useful techniques to utilize time effectively, avoid distractions, and keep procrastination at bay. So, let the clock ticking begin!

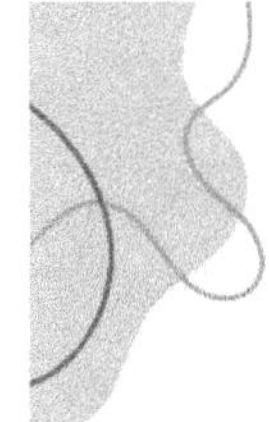

REFLECT &
STUDY

It's time to reflect on the study techniques and strategies covered in this chapter. Answer the following questions and assess your current study habits, identify areas for improvement, and set goals for becoming a more effective learner.

- Take a moment to think about how you study. What do you rock at? What could use some improvement?

  ____

  ____

- Have you ever found yourself getting lost in the abyss of social media while trying to study? Identify your biggest distractors and find ways to keep them at bay.

  ____

  ____

- Do you feel the urge to juggle ten things while studying? If so, how would you manage to focus better?

  ____

  ____

- Do you have a big school project looming? How would you chunk it into smaller and more manageable tasks?

  ____

  ____

- Is there any particular note-taking style that you like? Explore different note-taking styles and find the one that suits you best.

  ____

  ____

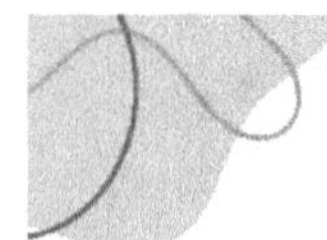

REFLECT &
STUDY

- Are you planning to conquer a tough test? Create a study plan using techniques like flashcards, practice problems, and maybe even a study group with friends.

____

____

- What are some cool study tools that you can use? Do you have a specific learning routine?

____

____

- Let's figure out which studying strategy works for you and how it will help you ace those exams.

____

____

- Review your latest study sessions – what went awesome? What could use a tweak? Apply your newfound knowledge next time to level up.

____

____

- Imagine explaining a tricky concept to a friend. How would you make it exciting and crystal clear?

____

____

- How many hours do you sleep? How can you ensure you are getting the quality sleep you need to crush it in the classroom?

____

____

- Summarize the key takeaways from this chapter in your own words. What are the most important things you learned about effective studying?

____

____

CHAPTER 3

Time Management & Organization Strategies: Essential Skills for Productivity

Have you ever heard the saying by Harvey Mackay, "***Time is free, but it is priceless. You can't own it, but you can use it. You can't keep it, but you can spend it***"? This is a powerful reminder of why time management is super important, especially for you guys. Your day is more like a limited-edition item, so once it is gone, you can't get it back.

Take the example of Nancy. She was a high school sophomore who loved spending time with her school friends, playing sports, and exploring her creative side through painting. However, Nancy often found herself overwhelmed with schoolwork and extracurricular activities, which left her feeling stressed and anxious. One day, Nancy had a major history project due, and along with a soccer game in the afternoon, she planned to hang out with her friends in the evening. Instead of managing her time effectively, she procrastinated on her project, spending hours scrolling through social media and watching

TV. She ended up pulling an all-nighter to finish her project, feeling exhausted and frazzled the next day. However, this could have been avoided with good time management, as it helps you make the most out of every moment.

By managing your time effectively, you can hang out with your friends, pursue hobbies, and chill out while spending much-needed time on school and academic activities. If you set aside some time each day for studying, you won't end up cramming the night before the test. This means less stress and better grades! And planning ahead for fun stuff means you can enjoy them without worrying about running out of time. So, remember, time management is not just about being strict; it is a way of giving yourself the freedom to enjoy life without all the stress!

When you manage your time effectively, you take charge of your schedule and priorities. This responsibility helps you develop independence as you learn to make decisions about how to use your time wisely. Instead of relying on others to remind you of deadlines or tasks, you become more self-reliant, which is a crucial skill for success in school and beyond. Time management is indeed a superpower when it comes to academic success. By mastering these skills, you can manage your study time, assignments, and projects efficiently while maximizing your productivity and focus. Moreover, when you know you have allocated enough time for each assignment or project, you can approach them calmly and confidently. This reduces anxiety levels, and that allows you to perform at your best without the added pressure.

And the great thing is that time management isn't just about academics; it is also about balancing your personal life. When you plan your time efficiently, you create space in your schedule for meaningful interactions with family and friends. Whether it is hanging out with friends, going on adventures, or simply having quality conversations, having more free time means you can nurture these important relationships in your life.

Good Time Management Skills

Imagine you are sitting in your room, panicking and freaking out about what to learn and what to skip for tomorrow's test. The clock is ticking, and you are getting anxious by the minute. Now you are thinking that all this nail-biting stress could have been prevented "only if I had studied throughout the week." But at that moment, you can't turn back the time! What you can do is learn and manage your time so well that you get to enjoy all your extracurricular activities while studying on a regular basis to avoid such last-minute panic. If you are thinking, how is that even doable? Then fret not! Here are some basic time management moves that you can easily learn to practice:

Plan, Plan, and Plan

Let's say you have a big science project due in two weeks. Instead of waiting until the last minute, you can plan ahead by breaking down the project into smaller tasks. For instance, assign one day for research and one for poster making, and practice your presentation a day before. You can employ this planning for any possible task, whether it's school projects, final exams, or sports activities. By planning what you need to do and when you will do it, you can avoid feeling overwhelmed.

Make checklists and to-do lists

These checklists and to-do lists are your lifesavers. When you create a list of activities you want to do, it helps you chalk out the perfect amount of time required to manage them in a day. Imagine you have a busy day ahead with homework, chores, and soccer practice. By writing down each task on a list, you can keep track of everything you need to do and make sure nothing slips through the cracks. Plus, there is something satisfying about checking off each item as you complete it! Here is a simple to-do list that you can copy and use to manage your daily tasks. It works best if you keep this list on your study table or desk- somewhere you can keep an eye on it. In this way, it will constantly remind you what you have accomplished and what needs to be done. This list works as a powerful reminder to keep you on track.

TO DO LIST

Day   Month

NO.	TO DO	Y / N
NOTES		

Set Your Goals - Big or Small

Whether it's getting an A on your history test or making your way into the soccer team, your goals define your day-to-day activities. Goals give you something to strive for and help you stay focused. Let's say you want to improve your grades in history. Setting a goal, like getting a B or higher on your next test, gives you a clear target to work towards your aim. You can then strategically break that goal into smaller steps, like studying for an hour each day or asking your teacher for extra help.

Set Your Priorities Straight

Priorities work like this powerful compass that helps you travel in the right direction. Not all tasks are created equal, and it is essential for you to know which ones need more of your attention and time. For instance, if you have a history test tomorrow and a movie night planned with friends, studying for the test has to be at the top of your priority list. This way, you make sure you are using your time wisely and getting the important tasks done. If you master the art of prioritization, it will help you a great deal in your professional endeavors as well.

Review and improve your workflows

Sometimes, it really helps to take a deep breath, step back, and look at how you are managing your time. Maybe you realize that you spend too much time chatting with friends during study sessions or that you are constantly getting distracted by your phone. By assessing your current workflow, you can come up with strategies to improve it and get more done in less time by avoiding unnecessary distractions.

Set thoughtful and practical deadlines

It is imperative to be realistic while setting your deadlines, as they can be your best friends or your worst foes, depending on how you approach them. Instead of waiting until the last minute to start a project, try setting deadlines for yourself along the way. This means that if you have a paper due in a month, you could set a deadline of one week for researching the topic, another deadline for writing the first draft, and a final deadline for editing and revising. By breaking down the project into smaller parts and setting practical deadlines for each one, you can avoid the stress of cramming at the last minute, which often negatively affects the quality of work.

Time Management Strategies

Now that you know what time management skills can do for you, it's time to delve deeper into some of the most effective and experts suggested time utilization techniques. You can use any of these strategies or a combination of one or two, depending on your requirements. But let me assure you. These tactics will not only help you manage time, but they can also help develop this great habit of focusing on one task at a time. Let's jump right in!

Pomodoro

In the 1980s, there was a guy named Francesco Cirillo. He was a university student at the time, and like most young adults, he was struggling with concentration and productivity. So, he came up with a technique, which he named after his tomato-shaped kitchen timer, "Pomodoro" (Italian word for tomato). According to Cirillo, if you break your work into short and focused intervals of activity separated by brief breaks, then you can get the task done successfully. Here is how you can employ this technique while studying or doing any other activity that requires your undivided attention:

1. First, set a timer. Choose a task you want to work on and set your timer for 25 minutes. If this duration seems too long initially, then you can begin with 10 or 15 minutes. This period of focused activity is called a "Pomodoro."

2. During each Pomodoro, focus entirely on the task at hand. Avoid all distractions and work with full concentration. During this time, you should have no cell phone around you, no constant pining of notifications or outside noise to distract you. If you are setting a timer on your cellphone, then make sure to keep it away from your sight and switch it to airplane mode.

3. When the timer stops and rings, take a short 5-minute break. Use this time to stretch, grab a drink, or do any other enjoyable activity to recharge your mind.

4. After this quick break, restart another Pomodoro session by setting your timer for another 15 or 25 minutes and continue studying. Repeat this cycle of focused work followed by quick breaks.

5. You can take a longer break of 15-30 minutes to relax after completing four Pomodoro sessions. Use this time to rejuvenate before starting the next set of Pomodoro.

To keep track of your Pomodoro activity per session or throughout the day, you can use the following Pomodoro tracker. Every time you finish a Pomodoro session for a certain activity, tick each circle given under Pomodoro sessions until the whole task is completed.

POMODORO TRACKER

DATE: _______________   DAY: _______________

TASK	POMODORO SESSIONS	DONE

REMINDERS & NOTES

____

____

____

The Eisenhower Matrix

Also known as the urgent, important matrix, this is a technique that is associated with Dr. Eisenhower, mainly due to his famous quote:

"I have two kinds of problems, the urgent and the important. The urgent are not important, and the important are never urgent."

This method is used to prioritize tasks at hand. It gives you a grid system to manage your work in an effective manner. Here is what this matrix looks like:

In the Eisenhower matrix, there are four quadrants that help you divide all your tasks into four different categories according to their level of urgency. This matrix is a great tool to prioritize your tasks and execute the ones that are most important while avoiding wasting precious time on activities that do not require your attention.

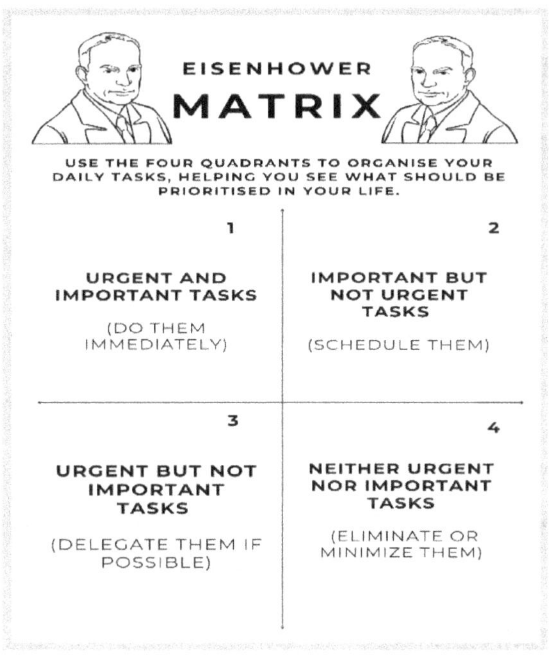

Time Blocking

It is a technique in which you divide the entire time of the day into several blocks and specify each block for a certain activity. For instance, you can allocate 4:00 pm to 6:00 pm for studying, 6:00 pm to 7:00 pm for dinner and 7:00 pm to 8:00 pm for relaxation. It is a simpler method that you can use to schedule your daily tasks. This way, you get to carry out all the activities throughout the day according to your workload.

The Two-Minute Rule

This rule is a quick way to complete small tasks at hand. According to this method, if you complete all the tasks that take two minutes or less, then you can actively prevent them from piling up. For instance, if you get an email asking a quick question, reply to it right away instead of leaving it for later. By tackling these small tasks as soon as they come up, you will keep your to-do list manageable.

Pareto Principle:

This principle is also widely known as the 80/20 rule. The proponents of this rule say that a person can achieve 80% of their results by putting in 20% of their efforts. This means that you only need to concentrate on the tasks that have the greatest impact on your final outcomes. For instance, if you are studying for a test, pay attention to the topics that are most likely to appear on the exam or the ones you struggle with the most. When you keep these high-impact tasks on top of your priority list, you maximize your productivity and achieve better results with less effort and in minimum time.

Batching Tasks

It gets easier to manage activities when you group similar ones together and complete them in one go. For example, instead of checking your email sporadically throughout the day, set aside specific time to do it, like once in the morning and once in the afternoon. This way, you reduce the time spent switching between different activities.

The Ivy Lee Method

The Ivy Lee Method is yet another technique for prioritizing your tasks and staying focused on what is most important. This method suggests creating a list of the six most important tasks every night for the next day. These tasks must be written in the order of their importance, with the most critical task at the top of the list. The next day, follow that list to start working on the tasks one by one and continue until they are completed. By following this method, you can make sure that you are always tackling the most important tasks first and making gradual progress towards your goals.

Identify Your Barriers

Do you find yourself constantly struggling against time? No matter how hard you try to manage, somehow, the clock ticks faster than your expectations, especially when you are doing last-minute exam preparation. It is often different time barriers that mess with your schedule and do not let you focus completely on a single task. Thus, they lessen your productivity. Let's address the three most common and most disruptive barriers that you will come across. And trust me! Once you learn to keep yourself away from them, your future self is going to thank you for your efforts.

Distractions

Every time you try to study with undivided attention and your phone keeps buzzing with notifications or your friends text you to hang out with them, you instantly lose focus. You pick up your phone, and just like that, you waste half an hour or more scrolling through your social media feed. Distractions like those are "time killers," and that's what they do! They disrupt your schedule and leave you struggling to manage multiple activities at once. Whereas, when you work in a distraction-free environment, you get the work done with greater productivity and in less time. Distractions come in all shapes and sizes. It could be the ping of a new message, the temptation of social media, or even just daydreaming instead of focusing on homework. They are everywhere, just waiting to catch your attention and throw you off the track. But fear not! There are ways to fight back and stay focused.

A few years back, I once met Sarah, who shared her high school experience! She was a bright young high school student. During her final year, she used to spend hours on her phone each day. Her grades started to go down, so much so that she feared failing her finals. Then, one day, out of this fear, she pledged to implement a digital detox and strictly followed a daily study schedule. Just like that, within 2 weeks of practicing this regime, she regained control of her time and saw a significant improvement in her grades.

- ***Cell Phones and Web Blockers***

That cell phone in your hand and the internet are two major sources of distraction in this age. The best way to avoid using a cell phone and constantly checking notifications during the study session is to install apps or web blockers that temporarily restrict your access to social media, gaming sites, or other distracting websites. You can try apps like "Forest or Freedom" that allow you to set timers for focused study sessions without access to distracting mobile applications or websites.

If the web blockers do not work for you, then keeping your cell phone away from your sight is the best technique. You can even leave your cell phone in another room so you are not tempted to reach for it every few minutes. Leave your phone in the kitchen or living room while you study in your bedroom so you are not tempted to check it every time you hear a notification. This technique works like magic when you are trying to break the habit of constantly using your cell phone.

- ***White Noise or Soft Music***

If random noises distract you while studying or doing your homework, then playing white noise or soft instrumental music in the background to drown out any distracting sounds is a great idea. Such music can create a more conducive study environment. Alternatively, you can use instrumental music or nature sounds and hear them through noise-canceling headphones while studying to block out background noise and stay focused. However, this technique only works for those who can concentrate while listening to soft or white music. So, only try if it works for you. If it doesn't, then choose a secluded and noise-free space in the house to study.

- ***Take Study Breaks***

You feel tempted to use a cell phone during the study session when you do not take breaks and get exhausted. If you give your brain a break every now and then, it will be easier for you to stay away from distractions during the study session. So, schedule short breaks during those sessions to recharge your batteries and prevent boredom, as we have already discussed in the previous section (Pomodoro technique). After studying for an hour, you can take a complete 10-minute break to stretch, relax your mind, get a snack, or go for a quick walk outside.

Overscheduling

Squeezing in too many activities in a set time frame is what overscheduling is all about. When you do so, it does more harm than good. It is so exhausting that it compromises the quality of every single thing you do. Let's assume you wake up early in the morning feeling tired because you stayed up late trying to finish your homework. You rush to get ready for school and grab a quick breakfast on the go. At school, you are bombarded with classes, assignments, and extracurricular activities. After school, you have sports practice, and then you go to music lessons and tutoring. With so much going on, you schedule a gaming session with your friends on the same day. What do you think could happen? By the time you get home, it will be already too late. You will hardly have enough time to eat dinner before collapsing into bed. And this cycle of exhaustion will continue the next day. So, when you are overscheduled, you are constantly rushing from one thing to the next, leaving little time to relax or recharge. This can result in excessive stress, burnout, and even physical health problems. So, it is super important to find a balance between pursuing your interests and goals and taking good care of your mental and physical well-being. Here is how you can avoid overscheduling on a daily basis.

- *Say "No"*

It is okay to say no sometimes, especially when you feel like you are taking on too much. If someone asks you to take on an extra project, stop for a second and think about whether you are capable of handling the pressure or whether it fits into your schedule and priorities. It is better to decline opportunities that will overwhelm you than to spread yourself too thin. Let's imagine you have a big history test coming up, and you are already juggling school and extracurricular activities, but you have promised your friend that you would join the drama club with him. Would you be able to manage preparing for a test while dedicating time to drama club? No! That is why you have to be quite selective about the tasks you commit to. Set some boundaries and refrain from saying yes to everything. If you are already juggling schoolwork, sports, and a part-time job, think carefully before agreeing to take on additional responsibilities.

- ***Create a Weekly Schedule***

Smart and practical planning is your savior here! See how much time you have available during the week and plan your daily activities according to the requirements. This practice can keep you from overcommitting. Use a handmade planner or digital calendar to map out your week and add school, extracurricular activities, work, and social events accordingly. This way, you can see where you might have multiple activities and make adjustments if needed. Every Sunday evening, take some time to review your upcoming week and block out time for all your commitments.

- ***Prioritize What Is Most Important***

When you have a lot on your plate, it is quite important to prioritize your tasks and commitments. Focus on activities and responsibilities that align with your goals and values and let go of those that don't contribute positively to your life. If you have a big test coming up, prioritize studying over hanging out with friends or watching TV. Remember that it is okay to put your academic and personal well-being first.

- ***Schedule Free Time***

Dedicating some time for relaxation and self-care amidst your busy schedule is a must. There is nothing wrong with taking a pause and enjoying some free time each day to unwind, recharge, and do activities you like, whether it is reading a book, going for a walk, playing with friends, or spending time with loved ones. Spare an hour each evening to relax and unwind before bed.

- ***Use Apps as Reminders or Notifications***

Technology can be a really useful tool to organize and manage your time effectively. There are mobile applications, or as we call them, "digital tools," which you can use to set reminders for important tasks, deadlines, presentations, and appointments. This way, you will be less likely to forget important commitments and can stay on track with your schedule. Google Calendar and To do list are two great tools that can help you stay organized and on top of your schedule.

Procrastination

Edward Young once said, "***Procrastination is the thief of the time***," and that couldn't be more accurate. It surely steals your time and energy and leaves you stressed out, scrambling to finish tasks at the last minute. When you procrastinate, all your important chores and schoolwork pile up. This can result in poor-quality work, missed deadlines, and added stress. Of course, nobody likes having a backlog of work, yet we all can get trapped in the lure of procrastination. How exactly? Well, sometimes, when we feel overwhelmed by the size of a task, like writing a long essay or studying for a big test, we tend to run away from it. Other times, it happens because we find the task too boring or challenging, so we put it off and indulge in more enjoyable activities.

For instance, you might procrastinate cleaning your room because it feels like a huge chore, or you may delay studying for a test because the subject is really difficult or simply a snore-fest. Whatever the reasons may be, procrastination can hold you back from reaching your full potential and achieving your goals. Luan, a recently graduated high school student, shared his experience.

"I tend to delay my school assignments and other tasks I need to complete. I end up wasting time on unimportant things until I'm under pressure to finish my assignment, which isn't the most effective time management strategy."

So, it is important to understand its harms and pledge to avoid it. Some effective ways to keep procrastination at bay are:

- ***Divide Large Tasks into Smaller Objectives***

Remember how we talked about "chunking" in the previous chapter? The same technique can be employed to avoid procrastination. Since big tasks are overwhelming, the best approach to deal with them is to divide them into smaller and more manageable targets. This makes them less daunting and helps you tackle them one step at a time. If you have a research paper to write, break it down into smaller targets, like researching your topic first, then outlining your paper, writing each section, and finally editing and revising.

- ***Different Strategies for Tackling Different Tasks***

Not all tasks require the same technique and approach. For some projects, it is more effective to start with the hardest or most unpleasant parts first, while for others, it might be better to begin with the easier or more enjoyable aspects. If you have a math assignment and a history essay to complete, you might choose to tackle the math assignment first since it is more challenging for you. Alternatively, if you find history more enjoyable, you could start with the essay to get into a productive mindset before moving on to math. Go with the strategy that works best for you. For instance, I often choose to do easier tasks at first to keep myself engaged, and then I switch to the harder parts gradually.

- ***Use Rewards as Motivators***

Rewards are a great way to keep us motivated. If you give yourself something to look forward to once you have accomplished a task or reached a milestone, you will feel more excited to get the entire work done. Rewards are powerful motivators that keep you focused and on track. If you finish your homework before dinner, reward yourself with some free time to play video games, watch a TV show, or chat with friends.

Maya, a high schooler, used to set a reward to motivate herself. Whenever she finished her history project before dinner, she could play basketball with her friends afterward. This gave Maya something to look forward to and helped her stay focused on her work. Maya worked diligently, and by dinner time, she had completed her project and enjoyed a fun evening shooting hoops with her friends. This shows how setting rewards can keep you motivated and focused on your tasks.

While it is great to reward yourself with some leisure time after completing your homework, it is important to keep time management in mind. Set a reasonable time limit for activities like playing video games, watching TV shows, or chatting with friends so you don't lose track of time and end up neglecting other responsibilities or commitments. Balance is key here!

- ***Create Artificial Deadlines in Advance***

"Work expands so as to fill the time available for its completion."

C. Northcote Parkinson

Have you ever heard about Parkinson's law? Those above words by Parkinson became the basis of this law, which says that the more time we give ourselves to complete a task, the longer it will take to finish it. On the other hand, if we set a smaller and limited time frame to complete the same task, we can manage to get it done quickly. So, it is true that procrastination often thrives when there is no sense of urgency. That is why you need to create artificial deadlines before the actual due date to create a sense of urgency and motivation to get started earlier. If your history project is due in two weeks, set a personal deadline for completing the research and outlining phase within the first week. This way, you will have more time for revisions and edits before the final deadline.

Organize to Thrive- Achieving Balance and Control

Do you want to know another intelligent hack to save your precious time and manage it wisely to get your important tasks done? Keep things organized! That's right. This may not sound fancy, but living in a mess-free and well-organized space can save you a lot of time.

Think about it! When you are desperately looking for your favorite shirt to go for a last-minute hangout with friends, but all your clothes are spread all over the floor, books piled up on your desk, and random stuff scattered everywhere, isn't that stressful? It takes forever to find that t-shirt, leaving you tearing through your closet like a madman. Whereas, if you keep your room neat and organized, you can effortlessly pull out your favorite shirt from a neatly folded drawer, and that only takes a minute or less. Keeping things neatly organized not only saves your time but also keeps your mind free from unnecessary stress.

Neatness is not just about appearances; it is more about making your life easier and more enjoyable. So, next time you are tempted to leave your room in a state of chaos, remember the benefits of keeping it neat and tidy. A neat space is like a breath of fresh air. Everything has its place, and you can easily find what you need without having to dig through piles of stuff. It is organized, clean, and inviting.

On the other hand, a messy space is like a jungle. Stuff is everywhere, and it is hard to find anything in that chaos. It can feel overwhelming and stressful, and it is not exactly a place where you would want to hang out. Perhaps there are several benefits of keeping your space clean and organized, such as:

- It boosts your mood. Believe it or not, a tidy space can actually make you feel happier and more relaxed. When your room is clean and organized, it is easier to focus and unwind after a long day. Plus, you will feel a sense of accomplishment knowing that you have arranged your stuff together.

- It also improves productivity. Whether you are studying for exams or working on a creative project, a clutter-free environment can help you stay focused and productive. With fewer distractions around, you will be able to concentrate better and get stuff done more efficiently.

And let's face it, your parents probably nag you about cleaning your room from time to time. But by taking responsibility for your space and keeping it tidy, you will be showing them that you are responsible and capable of taking care of your things. Also, it will earn you some brownie points!

Now that you know that an organized place is bliss, let's talk about the "how." Though it seems like a colossal task to clean your super messy room, if you are smart and strategic about it, you can definitely do it with ease. You don't have to clean the mess at once. Instead, divide and conquer! Start by cleaning and organizing one part or cupboard in the room, then move on to the next. Here is how you should begin!

Set Clear Expectations

Firstly, start by figuring out which stuff is important to you and why. Is it the pile of books at your desk that needs organizing so that you can start studying soon or the pile of clothes on the chair that needs to be folded first? With the order of priorities and goals in mind, you make a plan with specific tasks, such as tidying up the room or organizing your closet. But wait! You don't have to go overboard with it. Only set small goals you know you can reach. And remember, it is okay to change your plan if something is not working out for you. With dedication and a little flexibility, you will have your space in top shape in no time!

Create Systems

Have you ever been to a factory visit? A single product passes several stages, starting from putting together raw material to the final packaging stage. In every factory, you see multiple systems working in sync to produce tons of products in minimum time. That is the power of systematic production. The same is true when it comes to keeping your space neat and organized. If you have a system in place, then you can arrange everything in perfect order. Let me give you some ideas:

1. *Categorize Your Stuff:* One basic way to organize is to categorize your belongings into different groups based on their type or function. For instance, you can separate your clothes into categories like tops, bottoms, socks, and outerwear. Specify a designated space inside your cupboard for each category. Similarly, you can categorize books by subjects and gadgets by their functionalities. This way, you will have a clearer understanding of what you own and where everything belongs.

2. ***Use Containers and Bins:*** Once you have sorted your belongings into categories, consider using containers or boxes to keep similar items together. For instance, you can use those drawer organizers to keep your socks in different portions. For cupboards, you can buy wardrobe organizers to keep your shirts separate from jeans and other bottoms.

3. ***Designate Specific Areas:*** Scan your room for a minute and see which space is best for which stuff. There has to be a designated study area with a desk and shelves for school-related materials and a corner for sports equipment like basketballs or yoga mats. With dedicated spaces for specific purposes, you can streamline your routine and reduce the chances of clutter accumulating elsewhere.

4. ***Use Labels and Color-Coding***: Don't want to spend time thinking about which organizer carries which piece of clothing? Well, you can put labels and color coding to use! Label your shelves, drawers, or bins with the contents inside to make it easier to locate items quickly. Use different colored papers for each category and stick them outside the boxes, organizers, or containers.

I know a young and talented high school student, Alex, who has always prided himself on his sharp intellect. However, despite his intelligence, he struggled to keep track of his assignments and materials. One day, as he hurriedly rummaged through his cluttered backpack, panic washed over him. He realized he had misplaced his history essay, due in just a few hours. Frantically retracing his steps, Alex recalled the chaotic morning rush where he hastily stuffed his backpack with loose papers and textbooks. In his disorganized frenzy, the essay must have slipped through the cracks. With sweat appearing on his brow, Alex went back to his classroom, hoping against hope to find his missing assignment. As he entered the classroom, his heart sank. Papers were strewn across desks, and the room bore witness to the morning's flurry of activity. Desperation turning to determination, Alex began methodically searching every nook and cranny. Finally, buried beneath a pile of discarded worksheets, he spotted a crumpled paper—the elusive history essay. With a sigh of relief, Alex retrieved his assignment and went to his next class, his heart still racing from the close call. However, this experience served as a wake-up call for him. From that day forward, he vowed to take control of his organizational habits.

Inspired by his near-miss, Alex created a system of color-coded folders for each subject and designated compartments in his backpack for textbooks and loose papers. With this newfound discipline, he found that keeping track of assignments became second nature. No longer did he fear the chaos of a cluttered backpack or the stress of misplaced papers.

5. ***Set Regular Decluttering Sessions***: The more frequently you do the cleaning, the easier each session will get. Make it a habit to regularly declutter your space and remove items you no longer need or use. Set aside time every few weeks to check your belongings and decide what you would like to keep, donate, or discard. Decluttering not only prevents unnecessary accumulation but also makes sure that your space remains functional and clutter-free.

Use Storage Solutions

Your organization system won't work if you don't have a proper storage space in your room. I get it! It is easier to put everything in place when you have lots of free space in the cupboards, but when you have a small room with limited space in the cupboards, then organization becomes a hassle. Some smart ways to increase the existing storage space include:

- ***Shelves and Cubbies:*** Install shelves or cubbies on your walls to keep books and school supplies or even display your favorite items like trophies or collectibles. They are super handy and add a touch of personality to your room.

- ***Under-bed storage:*** Don't let that valuable under-bed space go to waste! Invest in some under-bed storage bins or drawers to stash away things like shoes, extra bedding, or seasonal clothes. It is a sneaky way to keep your room clutter-free.

- ***Over-the-Door Organizers****:* Maximize door space with over-the-door organizers. They are perfect for storing accessories, toiletries, or even snacks (yes, snacks!) without taking up any floor space. Plus, they come in funky designs to match your style.

- ***Storage Ottomans:*** Level up your seating game with a storage ottoman. Not only does it provide a comfy spot to sit, but you can also lift the lid and tuck away blankets, gaming gear, or anything else you want out of sight.

- ***Hanging Closet Organizers****:* Keep your closet in check with hanging organizers. They are great for storing shoes, folded clothes, or accessories like hats and bags. Plus, they come in multiple funky colors and patterns to jazz up your closet space.

- ***Drawer Dividers:*** Organize the chaos in your drawers with some handy dividers. Separate socks from your undies, or keep your desk drawers neat and tidy with compartments for pens, sticky notes, and all your other school supplies.

How to use a weekly organization checklist?

One fantastic tool that can help us stay on track is a weekly organization checklist. This checklist is like our personal assistant, reminding us of what needs to be done and when. It is a game-changer for managing our workload, making the most of our time, and keeping things in order.

- ***Choose or Create a Checklist:*** The first step is choosing or creating a checklist that works for you. You can use templates such as the one given below or even make your own using apps or good old pen and paper. The key is to find a format that you enjoy using, and that fits your style. Some prefer digital checklists they can access on their phones, while others like the satisfaction of checking off boxes on a printed sheet.

ORGANIZATION CHECKLIST

- ***Identify Your Key Categories:*** Once you have your checklist ready, it is time to identify the key categories you want to include. These categories will vary depending on your lifestyle and priorities. For example, you might have sections for schoolwork, chores, extracurricular activities, self-care, and personal projects.

- ***Do not forget about the Recurring Tasks:*** These are the things you need to do regularly, like homework, laundry, or exercise. Make sure to include them in your checklist, preferably under each relevant category. By scheduling these tasks into your weekly plan, you create a perfect routine that helps you stay on top of things without feeling overwhelmed.

- ***Use Notes or Additional Sections:*** Lastly, don't forget to leave space for notes or additional sections on your checklist. This is where you can jot down reminders, ideas, or anything else you need to remember. Maybe you want to add a section for meal planning or budgeting, or perhaps you need space to write down random thoughts or goals for the week.

Organizing Your Schoolwork

Trust me, I get it! Keeping track of assignments, projects, and tests can be overwhelming. But this is where a little organization can help you reduce stress, stay on top of your workload, and even improve your grades.

- ***Determine Task Priority:*** First things first, let's figure out which tasks are the most crucial and time-sensitive. Take a look at your syllabus, planner, or online school platform to see what assignments, tests, or projects you have coming up. Look for those that are due soon or carry the most weight in terms of grades. These are your priority tasks and should be at the top of your list.

- ***Sort by Priority and Due Dates:*** Once you have identified your priority tasks, it is time to sort them according to their importance and due dates. You can use a planner, calendar app, or even a simple to-do list to organize your assignments. Make sure to jot down the due dates for each task and arrange them in chronological order. This way, you will know exactly what needs to be done and when.

- ***Use the OHIO Rule:*** OHIO here stands for "Only Handle It Once," which means when you have a task to do, for instance, replying to an email, doing homework, or filling out paperwork, try to do it right away. Don't procrastinate or leave it for later. By dealing with it once, you save yourself from having to come back to it multiple times.

Cheers! You have made it to the end of yet another chapter. Here, we have addressed the most pertinent problem for teens in this era, "the struggle against time." There were lots of tips, techniques, and tools that would help you utilize and invest your time in healthy and constructive activities. It is said that "time is money" and I think you would agree with that. The best way to put this currency to use is to schedule your daily activities, use planners or online tools to create a plan, and then execute it by staying mindful and vigilant. After discussing all the time-saving strategies, we then went ahead to explore the benefits of organization and keeping a neat space. Whether it is your school work, the clothes in your cupboard, the books on your shelves, or the pens on your study table, the more organized they are, the easier it gets to use them. We discussed different methods to keep every aspect of your life organized. You just need to be consistent in your approach and continue tracking your progress to adjust your strategy when needed.

And now that your studies, school life, and rooms are all sorted, we are about to explore the most significant part of your lives - the bond and relationships you share with others, whether they be with your friends, family, relatives, or others around you. Those around us leave a lasting impact on our mindset and thought process, so we need to be intentional about our interactions with others. Keep in mind that the art of communication opens the door to healthy and effective dialogue, which leads to better understanding.

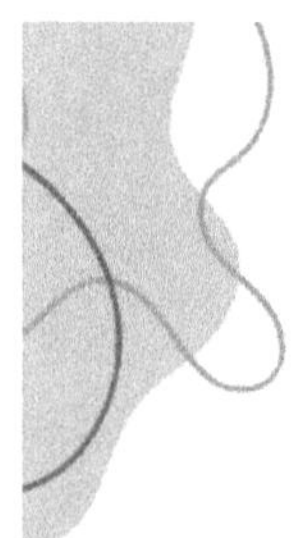

THE HOURGLASS SESSION

- How do you currently manage your time? Are you satisfied with your current approach, or do you feel like there's room for improvement?

- What are your biggest time wasters throughout the day? How can you minimize or eliminate these distractions?

- Can you identify any patterns in your daily routine that could be optimized for better efficiency?

- How do you prioritize your tasks and responsibilities? Are there any areas where you struggle to decide what to tackle first?

- What strategies or techniques have you found most effective for staying organized and on track with your goals?

CHAPTER 4

The Art of Connection Successfully Communicate and Build Relationships

"Nothing in life is more important than the ability to communicate effectively."

– Gerald R. Ford, former United States president

That's how important words are - they have the power to make you or break you. Using the right words at the right time makes any communication effective. Communication is not merely about exchanging words; it is how well you convey your thoughts, ideas, and emotions clearly and accurately. It is a two-way process that requires you to listen actively, understand other's perspectives, and respond thoughtfully. It is a means of developing mutual respect, trust, and meaningful connections. It empowers you to express yourself confidently, collaborate harmoniously, and resolve conflicts. Good communication can do so much more, such as:

- Good communication lays the foundation for building healthy relationships. It brings you closer to the people who really care about you. Whether it is your parents, siblings, relatives, or friends, you can enjoy their unwavering support and become the coolest version of yourself through open, honest, and constant communication. That is the magic of healthy relationships! They consistently boost your self-esteem and give you the courage to take on the world with a smile.

- Emotional Rollercoaster? Not Anymore! You will have a squad that always has your back, no matter what. Healthy relationships are anchors for emotions. The support system around you - your family and friends, can keep you grounded and help you ride out life's ups and downs without feeling like you are on a rollercoaster. With your crew by your side, every day feels like a victory.

- If you ever want to master the art of socializing, healthy relationships can be your secret weapon! Your loved ones can teach you how to talk, listen, and connect with others in ways that make you stand out from the crowd.

- Life can sometimes throw crazy curveballs at you, but with strong support and a relationship at your back, you will always bounce back like a champ. These connections act like your personal cheerleading squad, which gives you the power and resilience to tackle any challenge that comes your way.

Communication Styles

You see, there are different ways you can communicate with others, and the style you choose can have a big impact on how your conversation plays out. Whether you are being passive, aggressive, passive-aggressive, or assertive, each style has its own significance, and that can lead to different outcomes. The key is to recognize which style is most appropriate for the situation and adapt accordingly.

- **Passive Communication:**

Let's assume you are in a group project at school, and your classmates are making decisions without considering your opinions. Instead of speaking up and expressing your ideas, you stay quiet and go along with whatever they say, even though you are not happy with the direction the project is taking. This is what passive communication looks like. While being passive may seem like the easiest option in the short term, it can ultimately harm your relationships and prevent you from getting what you want or need.

- **Aggressive Communication:**

It is the complete opposite of passive communication. In an aggressive communication style, you use intimidation and hostility to assert dominance and control, which might be offensive to others and even make others avoid sharing their thoughts with you, and that makes the whole communication ineffective. While aggression may temporarily get your point across, it damages your relationship with others and creates long-term resentment and conflict.

- **Passive-Aggressive Communication:**

Then comes the mix of both, "Passive-Aggressive" communication. In this style of communication, you indirectly express negative feelings or resentment through subtle behaviors or comments. You avoid direct confrontation but express your frustration in a passive-aggressive manner. While it may seem less confrontational than aggression, passive-aggressive behavior can still harm your relationships and create tension. How so? Well, you are still not communicating your concerns with the other parties involved, which leaves them confused and unaware of the problems you are facing. It creates more confusion and misunderstanding and yields no effective results.

- **Assertive Communication:**

In contrast to the passive-aggressive style, if you openly share your thoughts and opinions with others without being impolite or rude, then you can truly assert yourself. Your assertive communication style helps improve collaboration and mutual respect among group members. It keeps the confusion and misunderstanding at bay. Plus, you get to solve all your conflicts in a friendly manner without hurting anyone's feelings or suppressing your own thoughts.

Overcoming Your Communication Barriers and Challenges

Bethany, a high schooler, once commented when I asked about her amazing communication skills:

"Mastering communication with others is more like picking up a new language. Initially, it is super challenging, but through dedication and practice, you can definitely improve."

Understanding a communication style is one thing, but practically employing those techniques in real-life scenarios is the real deal. Let's say you want to communicate your certain needs to your parents but fear getting snubbed in the process, or you want to share your thoughts with your peers but are afraid of their judgment. It all depends on the situation you are stuck in and how smartly you deal with it. A lot of the success of your communication depends on your perception of the situation and how you decide to convey your thoughts at the moment. Here, we will look into all the real-life communication challenges that most teens go through, and together, we will find their solutions:

Being an Introvert

Do you find small talk awkward or uninteresting? Do you feel more comfortable expressing yourself through writing than speaking? Do you feel overwhelmed or anxious in highly stimulating environments, such as crowded parties or events?

If your answer to those questions is yes, then, my friend, you are definitely an introvert. I feel your pain as I once dealt with the same. Communication is not a piece of cake when you are an introvert. It is rather a struggle that makes you anxious and often stressed. Face-to-face communication is the hardest of all, through no fault of your own. Words do not just come naturally to your mind when you are communicating with someone. But that's fine! You can work on your shyness, hesitation, and speaking skills to make daily social interactions less painful. How can you do that? Here are a few conversation hacks that will come in handy for you!

1. As an introvert, you hate small talk, so instead of having formal conversations with people you don't know, engage in deep and meaningful conversations with those you vibe with or feel most comfortable with.

2. Talking to a large group of people can be really intimidating, so start small and practice face-to-face communication with one or two people at a time. Then, gradually add on people as your comfort level begins to rise.

3. Prepare ahead! Though practically it is not always possible to anticipate every other interaction and prepare for it, but whenever you get the chance, ready yourself for it. Let's say you have this class discussion or a group meeting; think about all the possible topics that will be discussed, and brainstorm different ideas that you will feel comfortable talking about. Planning gives you confidence and limits the chances of that sudden "what do I say" panic attacks every time someone turns to ask your opinion.

4. Give yourself the space and time to counter your shyness and hesitation. If a certain gathering makes you feel uncomfortable, then take a break and enjoy some alone time. Return to talking only when you feel the energy to do so.

5. Lastly, do not compare yourself with extroverts around you. Yeah! Sometimes, it does feel like, "Only if I were an extrovert, life would have been much easier," but that is not true. Extroverts also face challenges that are different than yours, like getting a little alone time to rejuvenate themselves or keeping people out of their personal boundaries. So, embrace and cherish yourself for who you are. You just need to be the best version of yourself.

Face to Face Communication

In this age of Snapchat and WhatsApp, most teens and young adults find face-to-face communication really dreadful. I have heard many teenagers saying things like Emily:

"When you speak in person, there's added pressure because you can't edit or delete what you say."

Or things like what Mark has said:

"Texting feels like watching a prerecorded program. While talking face-to-face is more like being in a live show. All I can think of when I talk is, don't mess up, Mark!"

It is true that pressure is real, but face-to-face communication carries more authenticity, and sooner or later, you will have to talk to people in person, whether it is your college or job interviews or discussions with your family, friends, and loved ones. Face-to-face communication has so many advantages that I find it not an option but a necessity to create healthy bonds in life. When you talk to people in person, you get to observe their facial expressions, hand gestures, tone of voice, or overall vibe, which makes it easier for you to decide if they are being authentic and genuine in their conduct and if you can rely on them to connect at a deeper level. Plus, face-to-face communication gives you enough room to express your true emotions and feelings without getting misjudged or misunderstood. However, if you find it difficult to talk to people outside your mobile phone's screens, then you can always practice face-to-face communication in person using the techniques shared in this chapter.

Starting a Conversation

It is always difficult to start a conversation with someone, especially when you are meeting them for the first time. Those awkward silences are really petrifying when you just can't find the right words to begin with. Fortunately, there are a few tricks to break the ice and get a conversation flowing with anyone. One good technique to break the ice is "asking questions." Sounds simple, right? It can be about anything related to the other person or something you both can relate to. You can ask questions like:

"How is life these days?

"I have seen this cool new show. Have you watched it?"

"Did you hear about that ……. (some recent happening)?

These questions can prompt a discussion regarding a topic that can turn an awkward silence into a one-on-one communication session. Try to use more of the open-ended questions like "What was your favorite part in that movie?" as they can create room for more discussion.

Remember, asking questions is a great way to begin a conversation, but while doing so, make sure to avoid becoming an interrogator. Don't ask too many questions or ask one question after another; this can make the other person really uncomfortable. Just use this trick to initiate a conversation and then let it be.

Digital Communication

Digital communication is the reality of this age. Half of your time is spent sharing memes with your friends, posting content online, commenting, and texting your peers, so you also need to be intentional about your digital communication. You cannot let cyberbullies bully you under the garb of anonymity or allow anyone to use your information and content against you. This means you have to be cautious while communicating with people on social media or any online platform. The things you say in real life are often forgotten by people in the long run, but content posted online can be stored and used to exploit you if it falls into the wrong hands. So, be smart about what you share and say online.

Communication with Parents

"I find it difficult to communicate with my father," sighs Alex, a teenager who struggles to connect with his dad. "Sometimes I try to talk to him, but he seems preoccupied with work or his phone."

Now Alex has three options.

A. To slam the door and storm off in frustration.

B. To not talk to his dad at all.

C. To wait for the right time and bring up this subject again to talk in detail.

Options A and B are often the paths most teenagers take out of rage and frustration, but they do more harm than good and create more distance. You see, your parents are the major source of unconditional love and support in your life, and their constant input is valuable. Even when you feel like they don't get you, they care a lot about you. That is why it is important to overcome any communication barrier with them, truly understand their struggles, and then communicate your feelings to them. If they seem caught up in work, then that's fine! Take a deep breath to calm yourself first, then try to see things from their perspective as well and find the right time to share your concerns calmly. If you think they don't give you enough time, simply sit with them and discuss your issues. There lies a generational gap between you and your parents, which often makes it difficult for you to understand them and for them to get you. But, with open and effective communication, understanding, and empathy, you can overcome that barrier and open your heart out to let them know how much you value them and their words.

Now that you have learned how to cope with the communication challenges, let's move one step ahead and master basic communication skills.

Master Essential Communication Skills

If you ever felt like you were not being heard or understood or you struggled to express yourself or connect with others, then you are not alone in this! The teenage years are difficult, and there is a lot that you need to learn before becoming a speaking Maestro. Communication can be tricky, but with the right skills, you can make it super effective. Have you ever found yourself in a situation where you are trying to tell your friends how you feel, but the words just won't come out right, or maybe you feel like your parents don't really get where you are coming from? That's where effective communication skills can help you. And here are a few things that you need to practice to master this skill.

- **Active Listening is Key**

Communication is a two-way street, and it is actually more about listening than speaking. If you are a good listener, then you can understand others better and express yourself in the most appropriate and effective manner. Active listening is pretty simple and does not require any special skill. You just have to stay present in the moment while talking to someone, make eye contact with them, nod your head to show that you are listening, and ask clarifying questions to show that you understand. Avoid interrupting or thinking about what you are going to say next while the other person is talking. Jack, an enthusiastic young high schooler who has first-hand experienced the challenges of teenage life, also believes that active listening really makes communication effective. He suggests:

"As the other person talks, really listen. Maintain eye contact. Nod when appropriate. Smile. People appreciate it when you acknowledge what they have just said."

- **Understand Nonverbal Communication**

Peter Ducker once said, "***The most important thing in communication is hearing what isn't said***." And that is so true! It is often the facial expressions, body language, and tone of voice of the person speaking that convey the actual sentiments behind words. They give you a lot of information that words alone can't. To understand nonverbal communication, you need to pay attention to the speaker's body language and facial expressions. For instance, crossed arms might indicate defensiveness, while a smile and open posture might indicate friendliness. Practice observing and interpreting nonverbal cues in everyday interactions to improve your understanding.

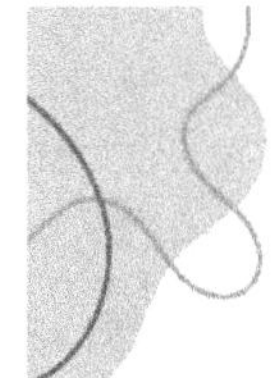

COMMUNICATION CHARADES

Communication Charades is a lively and entertaining activity designed to improve your communication skills through nonverbal cues and teamwork. You can play this game with your friends and even loved ones. Here is how you can play and learn to communicate while having a fun session filled with laughter!

- Divide all the participants into two teams with equal numbers of members. Each team will take turns performing and guessing the charades.

- Prepare a list of communication-related scenarios, phrases, or concepts for participants to act out. These can include common communication challenges, such as giving directions, expressing emotions, or negotiating conflicts.

- Each team takes turns and selects a member to be the "actor" while the rest of the team will have to be the "guessers."

- The actor silently selects a scenario or phrase from the list and begins acting it out using only nonverbal communication cues. They can use gestures, facial expressions, and body language to convey the message to their teammates.

- Meanwhile, the rest of the team observes the actor's movements and tries to guess the correct scenario or phrase within a specified time limit, typically 1-2 minutes.

- If the team successfully guesses the message before time runs out, they earn a point. If not, the opposing team has the opportunity to steal and guess the message for a bonus point.

- Rotate roles within the team so that each participant has the chance to be the actor.

- Continue playing rounds of Communication Charades, with teams accumulating points for each successful guess.

- After several rounds, tally up the points and declare a winning team based on the highest score.

Present Ideas Effectively and Confidently

Confidence can really amp up your communication game. Confidence is key to persuasion. Ask yourself! Who would you rather listen to a person who is confused and shy? Or someone who knows what he is talking about and says it out loud with confidence? Of course! Your attention will directly turn towards the latter; why is that so? Because that's how the human mind works. Confidence makes you more believable. You are taken seriously when you share your ideas in this way. To bring more confidence into your style of talking, start by organizing your thoughts and ideas in a clear and logical way in your mind. Use confident body language, such as keeping your posture straight and making eye contact with your audience. Practice speaking clearly by standing in front of the mirror to see what's missing and work on that to gradually improve your speaking skills.

- **Cultivate Empathy and Respectful Dialogue**

Empathy is the ability or skill to understand and acknowledge the feelings of others, and it helps you have a respectful dialogue with them. This skill is important because it helps to build strong and positive relationships with others. To develop empathy, you have to put yourself in the other person's shoes and imagine how you might be feeling if you were in the same situation as they are.

Let's say you are all dressed up, sitting, and waiting for your friend to go see a movie together. But your friend calls at the last minute to cancel the plan, saying he has caught some really bad flu. Now, this may be frustrating for you, and it might make you a little angry, but when you put yourself in your friend's place, you will understand what he must be feeling being down with the flu and fever. So, you will wish him good health without showing any sign of aggression. This compassion and empathy are a glue that binds people together and helps build meaningful relationships.

Building Meaningful & Healthy Relationships

Speaking of meaningful relationships, whether it is with your friends, family, or someone special, having them in your life is bliss. Through these relationships, you create your own squad, the people who get you and support you no matter what. But how can you define a meaningful connection? It is basically all about sharing laughs, having deep talks, and being there for each other through all the ups and downs. Such connections make life exciting and meaningful. So, let's understand together how we can create such beautiful bonds around us. Because, at the end of the day, it is these connections that make life truly special.

- **Be Authentic**

You don't need to mold and fold to fit in. It may seem like there is no other option when you are in high school, and you want to be seen as one of the cool kids, but when you pretend to be someone else just to make people like you, it shatters your inner confidence and self-esteem. That is why being yourself is the best way to connect with others. Whether you are into gaming, sports, music, or art, embrace what makes you unique. If you are passionate about photography, share your favorite shots with others and talk about what inspires you. Authenticity attracts genuine connections because that way, people can see the real you shine through.

- **See Things from Other's Perspective**

Sophia, a talented young high schooler, shared her thoughts, saying:

"I used to feel nervous when talking to others. Sometimes, I still do. But it helps when I take a genuine interest in the other person instead of focusing on my own insecurities."

And that is quite true! When you start focusing on others and their perspective, you tend to forget about your own communication inadequacies, and that makes it easier to talk. To make that happen, you will have to show empathy towards others while building trust and deepening your connections with them. If a friend is going through a tough time, listen to him without judgment and let him know you are there for him. Put yourself in his shoes and offer support and encouragement. Small acts of kindness can go a long way in creating meaningful bonds.

- **Shared Interests**

Finding common interests is a great way to bond with others. Whether it is playing video games, exploring nature, or binge-watching your favorite TV show, shared activities create opportunities for connection. You can join school clubs or groups that align with your interests as it helps you meet like-minded peers. If you are passionate about environmental conservation, join a local eco-club to connect with others who share your passion and values.

- **Attend Social Events**

Social events like parties, student seminars, discussion groups, school dances, or community gatherings are excellent opportunities to meet new people and form connections. Step out of your comfort area and strike up conversations with others. If you are at a school dance, ask someone to dance or join a group playing a game. Participating in such social events shows that you are open to meeting new people and can lead to meaningful friendships.

- **Cultivate Positive Attitudes**

A positive attitude can attract positive connections. Smile, be friendly, and approach interactions with optimism. Positivity is contagious, and people are drawn to those who radiate good vibes. If you are working on a group project, approach it with enthusiasm and encouragement. Your positive energy will inspire others and attract only those who share the same level of enthusiasm and encouragement, which later fosters a collaborative and supportive environment.

Avoid Misunderstandings

Have you ever been in a situation where you are talking and talking, but it feels like the other person just doesn't get what you are saying? Or do you feel like you are being misunderstood? Well, guess what? It happens to a lot of young adults of your age! Conflicts and misunderstandings in communication are totally normal, especially during those teen years when everything feels a little confusing. But it is all a part of growing up and learning through new experiences. There are tons of reasons why misunderstandings happen; it may be because of differences in perspectives, emotions running high, or someone just not being clear enough. But don't worry; there are tricks you can use to avoid those mix-ups and get your point across like a pro!

- **Be Precise and Unambiguous**

Clarity is one of the basic pillars of effective and meaningful communication. Be really specific while communicating about what you want or need. If you are making plans with your friends, instead of saying, "Let's hang out sometime," you should say something more specific like, "Do you want to go to the movies with me this Friday at 7?" This way, there is no room left for confusion about what you are suggesting, and your friends will know exactly what you are asking.

- **Focus on the Issue**

When you are having a disagreement or problem with someone, it is really important to stay focused on the main issue instead of blaming the other person. If you are arguing with your sibling about whose turn it is to do the dishes, instead of saying, "You never help around the house," you could say, "I feel frustrated when the dishes pile up, and I need some help." You see! This keeps the conversation focused on finding a solution instead of arguing about who is to blame.

- **Admit When You Are Wrong**

Sometimes, we make mistakes, and that is totally okay! It is a healthy trait to be willing to admit when you are wrong and apologize if you have hurt someone. If you accidentally break your friend's favorite mug, instead of making excuses, you could say, "I am really sorry I broke your mug. I will do my best to replace it." This shows that you take responsibility for your actions and care about other's feelings.

- **Avoid Over-Apologizing**

It is good to accept your mistakes and apologize when you are wrong, but over-apologizing is something that you should avoid as it shatters your self-esteem and confidence in the long run. Say you are running a few minutes late to meet your friend; instead of saying, "I am so sorry I am late! I am the worst," you could simply say, "Sorry I am late. Traffic was crazy." This way, you are acknowledging the inconvenience without overdoing it with apologies.

- **Use the "I Statements"**

When expressing your thoughts and feelings, the "I statements" work like magic. They stop you from blaming or accusing others while putting your point on the table. For instance, instead of saying to your friend, "You always ignore me," you could say, "I feel ignored when you don't respond to my texts." This way, you are expressing how you feel without putting the other person on the defensive. Shelly, a high schooler I met recently, shared her own experience, saying:

"During a group study session, my friends and I tackled a tough math problem. With differing ideas causing frustration, a friend skilled in communication suggested using an "I statement" to express thoughts calmly. This shift led to active listening, inclusion of diverse viewpoints, and collaborative problem-solving that highlighted the power of respectful communication."

So, yeah! That's how to avoid misunderstandings in communication and convey your ideas and thoughts in a manner that would really make an impact on others. Your communication skills are the sum of your speaking prowess, your gestures, your tone of voice, and the level of your confidence. Practice all of them, and soon, you will become the communication champ.

And that brings us to the end of this chapter. Here, we looked into some crucial interpersonal skills that are super important for your personal and social growth. We covered techniques for expressing your emotions and ideas honestly, understanding others' perspectives, and being a great listener. We also learned how being assertive and resolving conflicts positively can make your relationships stronger. So, who's ready to put these skills into action and level up their communication game? Let's check out the following reflective questions to assess your personal communication style and see what you have learned so far.

LET'S COMMUNICATE!

It's time to reflect on the communication strategies covered in this chapter. Answer the following questions and assess your current communication patterns, identify areas for improvement, and set goals for building strong and meaningful connections.

- How do you currently approach communication with others? Do you feel confident in your ability to connect with people and build relationships?

____

____

- Think about a time when you successfully communicated with someone and built a strong relationship. What strategies or techniques did you use in that interaction?

____

____

- How do you handle disagreements or conflicts in your relationships? Are there any communication techniques you could use to navigate these situations more effectively?

____

____

- Consider the people in your life who you feel closest to. What qualities or behaviors do they exhibit that contribute to the strength of your relationship?

____

____

- How do you express empathy and understanding in your interactions with others? Can you think of a time when showing empathy positively impacted a relationship?

____

____

CHAPTER 5

Teenagers and Financial Fitness Budget and Manage Money

"The safe way to double your money is to fold it over once and put it in your pocket."

- Kin Hubbard

You know what they say: "Save money, and the money will save you," that is quite actually true. Spending money mindlessly leaves you high and dry in your hour of need. Without savings, you are forced to rely on others or to step into the debt trap. But you can avoid that by being smart about your finances. Whether you get your allowance from your parents or you earn some bucks doing an after-school job, it is important to start thinking about how you manage your money, even if it is just a little bit. Sure, the money you receive might not seem like much right now, but learning to manage it early on can set you up for success in the future. Think of saving as planting seeds for a garden; the sooner you start, the earlier and better the harvest will be. Whether it is saving up for something you really want, budgeting for expenses, or even investing for the long term, every dollar you manage wisely now is a step towards your ultimate financial independence and security down the road.

Why Become Financially Savvy?

"You will either learn to manage money or the lack of it will manage you."

- Dave Ramsey

Now, you must be thinking, "Isn't money management something adults have to think about? Why should I start worrying about investment and saving when I don't even earn much?" Thoughts like these often run through most teenagers' minds. But the truth is, the sooner you start, the better it is. Stepping into adulthood without having learned the money management tricks is like going skydiving without knowing how to use a parachute. So, why wait till you turn 25 when you can start being financially savvy today? Those who learn to save and invest money from a very early age enjoy financial stability and security by the time they enter their late twenties. Think about it! When everyone else will be thinking about what to do with their lives and careers and dealing with financial crises, you will be running your own business enjoying your savings and investments. That is the power of starting early money and budget management.

Benefits of Saving Money

Benjamin Franklin once said, "***A penny saved is a penny earned***." Let's put this into perspective and assume you have been eyeing the latest gaming console for months. Finally, the day comes when it is released. Excited, you rush to the store, only to realize you don't have enough money to buy it. Disappointed, you walk away empty-handed, wishing you had saved up for it beforehand. This scenario shows why saving is crucial for you. By setting aside some amount of your earnings regularly, you can build up a stash of cash for those big-ticket items or unexpected expenses. Saving not only allows you to achieve your goals and dreams but also provides a safety net for emergencies. Plus, it teaches valuable lessons about financial responsibility and planning for the future. So, you must consider putting some aside for a rainy day so that your future self will thank you!

Ways to Save Money

Do you want to save money and keep some extra bucks for rainy days? There are lots of smart strategies that you can try. Let's find out!

- **Open a savings account**

If you are thinking about giving your money a cool place to grow, then a savings account is your best shot! It is your personal treasure chest, where you can keep and see your cash grow over time. Setting one up is super easy; you can just head to the bank with your parents, and they will help you get started. Once your account is up and running, you can deposit money whenever you want, and the bank even gives you a little bonus called interest. So, if you are dreaming of saving up for that awesome new gadget for college or a future adventure, a savings account is your ticket to making it happen!

But what if your family doesn't have much money or you live in a place where teens rarely have their own cash to spend? Even so, your family likely has some resources, no matter how small they may seem. In that case, spend or use those resources wisely because adopting a mindset of spending without thinking would be detrimental to you and your family's well-being.

- **Separate spending and savings money**

Say you have a wallet full of cash, but how do you know what is good for spending and what is for saving? You need to divide and conquer!

Set aside a portion of your income for spending on fun stuff like snacks or movie tickets and another portion for saving up for bigger dreams like a new bike or a trip with friends. This way, by keeping your spending and savings money separate, you will have a clear plan for where your money is going and avoid accidentally dipping into your savings when you don't really need to.

- **Keep track of purchases**

Have you ever felt like your money disappears faster than you can say "cash"? I experienced the same when I was in college. But when you keep track of your purchases, you become your own detective on a money mission! For this, you can create an expense tracker. Take a notebook or use your phone to jot down everything you buy, from that yummy smoothie to the latest game. At the end of the month, take a look at your list and see where your money went. Maybe you will spot some sneaky spending habits you can cut back on or find extra cash to add to your savings. You can create an expense tracker, as shown below, to track your spending and calculate the monthly total.

MONTH:

EXPENSE TRACKER

DATE	DESCRIPTION	CATEGORY	AMOUNT
		TOTAL	

- **Think twice before buying:**

You know that feeling when you are about to buy something and are unsure if you really need it? That's your inner money-savvy detective kicking in! Before you make a purchase, take a moment to ask yourself if it is something you truly want or just something you are buying on a whim. Use the **24-hour rule** to stop yourself from impulse buying. If you are eyeing that new pair of sneakers, then take 24 hours to make a final decision. This period is enough to logically analyze and practically think about the repercussions of buying an unnecessary, expensive item. By pausing and thinking twice before buying, you will make smarter choices with your money and have more cash left over for the things that really matter.

- **Do chores to earn more allowance money:**

Do you want to earn extra cash to help you achieve your savings goals? It is time to put your skills to work! Offer to do extra chores around the house, like washing dishes, mowing the lawn, or walking the dog. Not only will you help out your parents, but you will also earn some extra allowance money to put towards your savings. It's a win-win!

- **Get a summer or part-time job:**

If you are looking to boost your savings even more, why not consider getting a summer or part-time job? Even if it is babysitting, dog walking, or working at a local store, do it! Having a job can help you earn extra money to put towards your savings goals. Plus, it is a great way to gain new skills, meet new people, and have some fun while you are at it!

- **Set a savings goal:**

Do you dream big? Like getting into a highly prestigious college or starting a business at a young age? You can make all that happen by setting your savings goals. It is like giving yourself a roadmap to make it happen! Decide what you are saving up for. Having a specific goal in mind keeps you motivated and focused on your savings journey. It feels pretty awesome when you finally reach your goal and can enjoy the fruits of your hard work!

Ask your Parents

Your parents have been managing finances since way before you were born - they have been through a lot, and they know every little hack to save, spend, and invest the money wisely. You can ask them to share their pool of financial wisdom with you to help you sort out your money problems as well. You can gain valuable insights from their examples. Ask them about household expenses and how they manage their finances. What they are doing today will be your reality tomorrow. Soon after high school, you will be taking on those responsibilities, whether you live in college or somewhere else, so you must know how to spend wisely. Lisa used to consult both her parents to manage her finances, and now she has grown into a confident young woman. There is so much she has learned from her parents when it comes to money. She said:

"My dad taught me how to plan my money, and he showed me why it's important to keep things organized when handling family money. My mom taught me to check prices before buying anything. She was really good at making a little money, which went a long way. Now, I can take care of my own money because of what they taught me."

You can ask your parents the same; they will give you lots of amazing tips and tidbits that will help you throughout your adult life.

How do I Control My Spending?

"Buy now, think later." This one mindset can ruin your entire budget and leave you penniless at the end of the month. Of course, it is hard to resist when you see your favorite bag or shoes displayed at the mall or the coolest "skin" of your favorite video game is out in the market, but you can fight that thought and avoid impulse buying by being practical about it. It is possible to control your spending and enjoy your financial freedom at the same time.

"Sometimes, advertisers create a sense of urgency, making it seem like you must buy right away without any time to think. However, in most cases, you actually do have time to consider your decision. If you don't, it could be a hint that the purchase might not be wise." Riku, a marketing strategist, once shared his insights with me at a conference. According to him, most teens assume that by controlling their spending, they will be restricting their freedom, but that's a myth! When you control your spending and save money for the things that you really like, it grants you more freedom and financial security.

I get it. It is difficult to counter your spending urges and keep yourself from getting distracted, but there are some power moves that can keep your spending in control:

1. Create a practical and actionable budget plan that covers all your basic expenses (discussed in the next section).

2. Abandon the mindset of buying now and thinking later. Become a mindful consumer and think about the pros and cons of your purchases.

3. Avoid impulse buying by keeping your emotions in check. Sometimes, you really like something and just can't resist it. However, once you bring it home, you don't even find it that useful. So impulse buying leaves you empty-pocketed with things that you might not even like later. You can avoid this by waiting at least 24 hours or more before making the purchase. Use this time to think about the product, its price, and the value it provides. You might end up thinking differently.

Budgeting 101

Budgeting tells you where and how much money to spend in a given period of time. You make a foolproof plan to make the most out of every dollar. Sit down and decide how much you want to spend on different things each month, like snacks, clothes, and savings for the future. For example, if you get an allowance of $20 a week, you might decide to spend $5 on snacks and $10 on hanging out with friends and put $5 into your savings. By sticking to your budget, you will know exactly where your money is going and be able to reach your savings goals faster.

Take Mark, for example, a typical present-day high school junior. He landed his first part-time job at a local restaurant. With his new income, he started spending recklessly on eating out with friends, buying expensive gadgets, and going to concerts. However, he never bothered to keep track of his spending or set aside money for savings. When his bike broke down unexpectedly, he didn't have enough money saved up to cover the repair costs. Mark had to borrow money from his parents and was left with little to no savings. This served as a wake-up call for him, and he realized that if he had practiced budgeting and set aside a portion of his income for emergencies, he could have avoided this financial crisis. Soon, he started implementing smart techniques to save money, and his savings really helped him when he got into the college of his choice.

Keep it simple in the beginning.

New to budgeting? Don't worry! You can begin by taking small measures. Start by putting all your sources of income down in an organized list (allowances or part-time job earnings). Then, jot down your expenses. It is important to be realistic about what you spend money on. Once you have everything written down, subtract your expenses from your income to see if you are spending more than you are making. If you are, it is time to make some adjustments. Maybe cut back on non-essentials like eating out or buying new clothes. The goal is to make sure you are not spending more than you have. As you get more comfortable with budgeting, you can start adding more details and categories. But for now, keeping it simple will help you stay on track and in control of your finances.

You can create a weekly or monthly budget planner to write down your income, expenses, and spending goals. Let me show you a simple template here:

BUDGET
Planner

MONTH _______________

YEAR _______________

INITIAL BALANCE _______________   **ENDING BALANCE** _______________

INCOME

DATE	DESCRIPTION	AMOUNT
		TOTAL

EXPENSES

DATE	DESCRIPTION	AMOUNT
		TOTAL

SUMMARY

TOTAL INCOME	TOTAL EXPENSES	ENDING BALANCE

NOTES

____

____

____

____

Different budgeting methods

There are several other budgeting methods that you can employ to systematically save money without depriving yourself of the basic necessities.

- **Envelope method:** In this method, you make different envelopes for different expenses – for example, one for food, one for movie tickets, and one for saving up for something big. Each time you get some money, you divide it up among your envelopes. When an envelope is empty, you know you have spent all you can on that category. My daughter has been using this technique for budgeting since the age of 10, and now she is so well-versed in budgeting that she can quickly categorize and manage all expenses without even using any envelopes.

- **50/30/20 rule:** This rule is super easy to remember! You split your money into three categories: 50% of your money should be used for basic needs (like food and clothes), 30% for your wants (like going

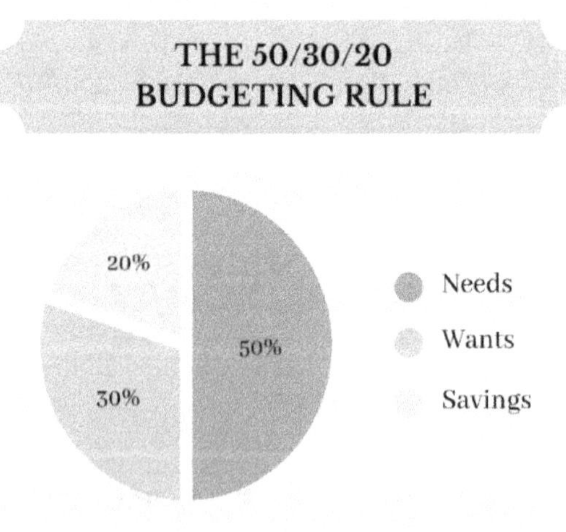

out with friends), and 20% for savings. It is a great way to make sure you are covering all your bases while still having some fun money to spend. This formula will help you throughout your adult life.

- **Zero-based budgeting**: In this method, you assign a purpose to every penny you earn. You start with your total income for the month and then allocate it to different categories like bills, savings, and spending until you have zero dollars left. It might sound a bit strict, but it helps you stay on track and make sure every dollar is working for you.

- **Digital budgeting apps:** If you are more into technology, there are tons of cool apps out there that can help you budget like a boss. Apps like Mint, YNAB (You Need a Budget), or Pocket Guard can track your spending, set savings goals, and even send you reminders to stay on track. In your country, there may be some other digital applications that are available, and you can use them as well. The goal is to organize your spending, record it, and keep track of it in any simple table.

- **The difference between wants and needs**: So, you are at the mall and eyeing that slick new pair of sneakers. Before you hit the checkout, ask yourself, "Is this something I want, or do I really need it?" Needs are the things that are absolutely vital for survival, like food, shelter, and clothes, while wants are the extras that make life fun but are not essential. When budgeting, prioritize your needs first and then see how much wiggle room you have for your wants. It is all about finding a balance between taking care of yourself and treating yourself.

Use budget categories

Budget categories help you organize your money into different groups based on what it is for. Start by listing out all your expenses into groups: groceries, transportation, and entertainment. Then, assign a specific amount of money to each category based on your income and priorities. This way, you will know exactly how much you have to spend in each area and can avoid overspending.

Make regular budget adjustments

Think of your budget as a living, breathing thing. It is okay to tweak and adjust it as needed. Maybe you get a raise at your part-time job, so you can afford to allocate more money to savings. Or you realize you are spending way too much on takeout, so you decide to cut back and reallocate that money elsewhere. By constantly reviewing and adjusting your budget, you will stay on top of your finances while making sure your money is working for you in the best way possible.

Establish Good Credit

Imagine you are 20 and ready to buy your first car. You head to the dealership, excited to pick out the perfect ride. But when you apply for a loan, the dealer tells you that your credit score isn't quite up to snuff. What is a credit score, you may ask? Well, it is more like a financial report that tells lenders how responsible you are with money. It is a big deal when it comes to borrowing money for things like cars and homes or even getting a new phone plan. Now, why should you care about your credit score? Think of it as your ticket to financial freedom. A good credit score can help you qualify for good interest rates on loans, get approved for an apartment, and even land your dream job. Here is how you can keep tabs on your credit score by making smart financial choices.

Go for student credit cards: Student credit cards are a much safer option than traditional credit cards, as they are specifically designed for college students and often come with lower credit limits and fewer fees than traditional credit cards. They provide an opportunity for students to build credit while still in school. When selecting a student credit card, look for one with features like no annual fees, rewards for responsible use, and educational resources to help you learn about credit management.

Get a secured credit card: When you use a normal credit card to buy stuff, you have to pay for the used amount with interest later. This approach is risky if you fail to pay the money back in a timely manner. However, when you use a secured credit card, you make a deposit upfront, typically equal to your credit limit. This deposit works as collateral and reduces the risk for the lender, making it easier for people with limited or no credit history to qualify. By using a secured credit card responsibly, you can make timely payments and keep balances low. This way, you can slowly build a positive credit history. Over time, as you demonstrate responsible credit behavior, you may become eligible for a traditional unsecured credit card with higher credit limits and more favorable terms.

Pay on time: Your payment history is one of the most significant factors affecting your credit score. When you pay your bills on time, it shows to the lenders that you are responsible and reliable. Late payments, on the other hand, will have a negative effect on your credit score and stay on your credit report for up to seven years. To avoid late payments, set up automatic payment systems or reminders to make sure you never miss a due date.

Use Credit Cards with Caution

When you have a credit card in your pocket, it can lure you into buying things and paying for them later. But do you know that when you buy multiple items and your credit starts accumulating over time along with interest, it becomes almost impossible to pay back the credit card bills in time? This delay in payment sets up a cycle of debt, which badly wrecks your credit score. Julia, a recent college graduate, opined:

"Being stuck in debt feels terrible. I have been there, and I never want to go back. Avoiding debt lets me grab opportunities and feel more at ease."

So, be really cautious while using a credit card. If you are not earning enough to pay your VISA bills later, then avoid using a credit card at all. Avoiding a purchase on credit or buying the thing in cash is better than dealing with the burden of debt later.

With that being said, we have now covered another major skill set- money management. The main aim of this chapter was to provide you with essential knowledge and practices for handling your finances wisely. We discussed the importance of budgeting, saving, and spending responsibly. Remember, setting financial goals is key to success! We also discovered the importance of assessing the difference between needs and wants and how saving for emergencies and future goals is crucial. My goal was to ensure that you have the tools and skills needed to make informed financial decisions throughout your life. Are you excited to put these money management skills into action? Let's begin!

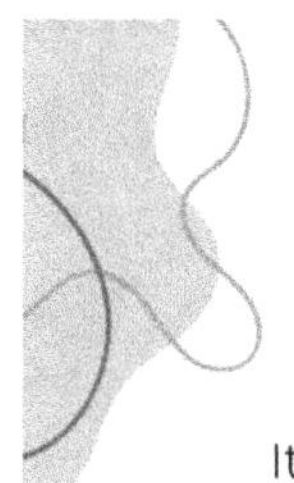

FINANCIAL HABITS AND GOALS

It's time to put on your thinking hats and answer the following questions!

- What are your current spending habits, and do you think they align with your financial goals?

- Let's imagine you have collected $500 from your monthly allowance, an after school job, and by doing some chores around the house. How would you divide it according to the 50/30/20 rule?

- Think about your long-term financial goals, such as saving for college or a car. What steps can you take now to achieve those goals?

- Reflect on the recent purchase you made. Was it a need or a want? How could you have used that money differently?

- Consider a time when you had to make a choice between spending money on something you wanted and saving it for the future. How did you make that decision, and do you feel satisfied with the outcome?

CHAPTER 6

The Power of Choice Developing Effective Decision-Making

"Every decision you make reflects your evaluation of who you are."

– Marianne Williamson

t is true that our life's journey is paved with choices, and each decision we make holds the power to shape our future. Making the right decision at the right time is a great skill that many of us rarely reflect upon. While it may seem that good decision-making power comes naturally to a person, that's not entirely true. Like any other skill set, it can also be polished through learning and practice. The more you learn and implement strategic plans to solve problems, the better your problem-solving skills become. This power works like a superhero cape that helps you sort out conflicts, be independent, achieve those big, audacious goals, and make decisions like a pro. See, during your teenage years, your brain works like a super sponge that soaks up all kinds of new knowledge and skills. And problem-solving? Consider it a workout for your brain, as it helps you grow stronger and smarter with each challenge you face.

Your Choices Matter

I once read a very inspiring book named "Man's Search for Meaning." A Holocaust survivor and psychiatrist named Viktor Frankl wrote it. His following words from the book really resonate with the idea of making choices, and they really touched me:

"Everything can be taken from a man but one thing: the last of the human freedoms — to choose one's attitude in any given set of circumstances, to choose one's own way."

That sums up the essence of our existence. We are all born with the freedom to make choices. Isn't it amazing? Critical thinking is one trait that makes us humans different from all other living beings on this planet. So, being able to think and decide what's the best course of action for you is a superpower that you all are naturally born with. You just have to find it inside you and put this ability to use.

You just have to be intentional with your decisions and take charge of your own happiness. Remember, every choice you make is like adding a piece to your life puzzle. You are the one putting it all together with the support and guidance of those who love you!

In your teenage years, you will constantly face several life-altering decisions, such as choosing the majors, selecting a college, opting for a profession, or doing a side hustle. This is the time when you need extraordinary decision-making skills, but unfortunately, it is also the time when your emotions are all over the place, and you struggle with several changes and identity issues. And that makes it really difficult to reach the right decision. This is where employing effective decision-making techniques makes life easier. They are beneficial in several regards, as they can help you:

To become independent: With your decision-making skills finely tuned, you can confidently make the choices that feel right for you. No need to blindly rely on anyone else's opinions.

To achieve even the most challenging goals: Armed with your problem-solving skills, you break down the goal into bite-sized chunks, brainstorm creative solutions, seek advice from mentors, and persevere through setbacks. Before you know it, you will be turning dreams into reality!

To choose and make decisions on your own: With your decision-making skills sharpened like a sword, you can confidently weigh your options, trust your instincts, and stand firm in your choices.

To sort out conflicts: When you put your problem-solving hat on, you calmly listen to other's perspectives, find common ground, and resolve conflicts with a cool-headed approach.

Challenges of Decision-Making & Their Solutions

Making a decision when you are torn between two really cool options is one of the hardest things that you will ever have to do. We all constantly come across such situations where it is difficult to rule out one option in favor of another, yet we have to decide as our future counts on it. If you really think about it, making a decision is not that difficult, right? You just have to weigh out the advantages and disadvantages of all the options and pick the one that suits you the most. Does that seem too hard? Of course, It does! In reality, there are several influences and external factors that may cloud our judgment and make us lose the ability to assess the situation practically. Often, you end up feeling like your mind and heart are at war with one another. The mind favors logic, and the heart brings desires and emotions into the equation, and you just can't decide what to do. Does that sound relatable? Well, at your age, there are several other challenges of such sorts, such as:

Peer pressure: You know how sometimes your friends want you to do stuff that you are not really comfortable with? That is called peer pressure. It can be tough to say no when your friends are all doing something, even if it doesn't feel right to you. But you can totally fight this pressure! If your friends are pressuring you to do something you are not comfortable with, it is essential to stand your ground. For instance, if your peers want to skip class and you know it is not right for you, you can say something like, "I appreciate the invite, but I need to focus on my studies. How about we hang out after school instead?" By setting boundaries and sticking to your values, you show that you are not easily swayed by peer pressure.

Strong emotions: Your emotions can be all over the place during your teenage years. Sometimes, they are so intense that they make it hard to think clearly. When you are feeling super emotional, it can be tough to make smart choices. When emotions are running high, it is often helpful to simply take a step back and analyze the situation calmly. Say you are feeling angry after an argument with a friend. Instead of reacting impulsively, take a few deep breaths and consider the best way to handle the situation. Maybe you decide to take a break and revisit the conversation later when you are both calmer. By regulating your emotions, you can make decisions that are more thought-out and less influenced by temporary feelings.

Lack of critical thinking: Your prefrontal cortex - the part of the brain that helps you think logically, is still developing, and it continues to do so until you are 25 years old. So, yeah! Though critical thinking is a superhero power for decision-making, at this stage, you are still developing and enhancing it. As a teen, you are learning how to use those powers. Sometimes, you might not think about all the possible outcomes before making a decision, and that's all right! Because that's how you learn. Developing critical thinking skills takes practice, so don't be too hard on yourself. Let's say you are trying to decide whether to join a club at school. Take the time to research the club's activities, talk to current members, and consider how it aligns with your interests and goals.

Information overload: Yuval Noah Harari, in his book "21 Lessons for the 21st Century," aptly says: ***"In a world deluged by irrelevant information, clarity is power."*** And that is so true! Today, you are constantly bombarded with information, scrolling through social media, watching television, movies, and whatnot. Think about all the stuff you see and hear every day on the internet. It is a LOT to take in! Sometimes, all that information can be overwhelming, and it makes it hard to figure out what to do. This information leaves no room for clarity and clouds your judgment. The solution? Let me explain through an example! If you are researching colleges and feeling bombarded by all the options, then instead of trying to process everything at once, break it down into smaller tasks. Start by making a list of criteria that are important to you, such as location, campus size, and academic programs. Then, focus on researching one criterion at a time to avoid feeling overwhelmed by the sheer volume of information.

Fear: This four-letter word has the power to wreck all your decisions if you let it consume you. It is totally normal to be fearful of the unknown and the future, but sometimes, it can get in the way of making smart choices. It sends your brain into overdrive and makes you think of all the things that could go wrong or the mistakes you would make. But the deal is that fear doesn't have to control you. Good or bad, you learn through your experiences, so don't let your fear hold you back. Try to negate those self-doubt thoughts. Even if you don't get a part in a play or pass an exam, you will gain valuable experience and build resilience along the way. Embrace the motto, as Susan Jeffers wisely said, ***"Feel***

the fear and do it anyway," as you deal with the challenges of decision-making.

Effective Decision-Making Strategies

When it comes to making decisions, you are not flying solo! There are strategies out there to help you navigate through the maze of choices life throws your way. You must have a treasure map to guide you and find the pot of gold at the end of the rainbow! These strategies are the tools in your toolbox, ready to be pulled out whenever you are faced with a tough decision. Whether it is weighing the pros and cons or thinking outside the box, these strategies can help you make the right decisions that may lead to success and happiness.

Do Not Rush into Any Decision

I understand it is super tempting to jump into things headfirst, especially when you are excited or under pressure. But you have to take your time to think things through and save a lot of trouble in the long run. Here, you can again use the **24-hour formula**. Take at least this much time to think before saying yes or no to an offer. For example, suppose your friends want to go on a road trip, but you are not sure if it is the right time. In that case, instead of saying yes right away, tell them you need time to think, then take a day or two to consider your schedule, budget, and any potential risks involved, and then answer them.

Do Your Research

Knowledge is power, right? Before making any big decisions, it is important to gather as much information as you can.

"The more you know, the better you can decide."

- Oprah Winfrey

Information gives you clarity and helps make the decision-making process much easier. If you are thinking about applying for a part-time job, then do some research on different job opportunities, read company reviews, and the application process. The more you know, the better equipped you will be to make an informed decision. Through this process, you will know if an opportunity really resonates with your needs and values.

Weigh All the Factors

Every decision has its pros and cons, so it is important to look into all of them before making up your mind. The easiest and most effective way to do so is to make a list of pros and cons and then compare the options. Let's assume you are trying to decide whether to join a sports team. In this case, you can think about how it will impact your schedule, your social life, and your overall well-being. By weighing all those factors, you can make a decision that aligns with your goals and priorities.

What If I Made a Bad Decision That I Cannot Change?

Rachel Golchin once said, ***"It's not how we make mistakes, but how we correct them that defines us."*** So yes! We all are bound to make mistakes because nobody is perfect, and there is no such thing as the "perfect decision." Sometimes, things do not work out in your favor, no matter how much effort you put into the decision-making process. But that's totally fine! Mistakes help you learn more, and they leave behind lessons that you will never forget. So, while you must take all the necessary precautions to protect yourself from any harm and avoid making mistakes, it is also necessary to be open to trial and error without beating yourself about it. It is all a part of the human experience.

Focus On Your Values- Avoid Comparison

You need to make decisions based on what is right for YOU, not what everyone else is doing. It is quite easy to compare ourselves to others, especially with social media painting a picture-perfect version of everyone's lives. But your values, aims, goals, and needs are unique to you. What works for someone else might not work for you, and that's totally fine! Whether it is choosing a career, deciding who to hang out with, or setting your personal goals, listen to the voice inside you and follow your own path. When you make decisions that align with your true self, you will feel more fulfilled and confident in the choices you make. Forget about keeping up with the Joneses instead, focus on being the best version of YOU.

And that's how you make a good decision! By considering all the factors involved. At the end of the day, the decision that aligns with your values is the best one. This reminds me of a quote I once read:

"Decision-making is easy when your values are clear."

– Roy Disney

Your values and ideals are your guiding light. If you know what you really want and your mind is clear about your goals, then nothing can stop you from making decisions that will serve you well in the future. You just need to have a belief in yourself and be patient, practical, and smart about it.

Keys to Problem Solving

"A problem is a chance for you to do your best."

- Duke Ellington

Every time you come across a problem, it presents you an opportunity to sharpen your problem-solving skills and make an upgrade in your life. Problems are inevitable, and we cannot keep running away from them forever. The best approach is to face your problems head-on and take proactive measures to solve them before they turn into a bigger crisis.

It is true that solving a complex problem might seem daunting at first, but trust me, you have what it takes to overcome any challenge that comes your way. Whether it is a tough math problem, a disagreement with a friend, or a big decision to make, remember that there is always a solution out there waiting to be discovered. So, don't be afraid to roll up your sleeves, get creative, and tackle those problems head-on. With a little patience, persistence, and a positive attitude, you will be surprised at what you can achieve. You just need to be strategic about it! Use the following key points to:

- **Clearly understand the issue**: You need to know what you are dealing with before you can crack the case! So, start by clearly stating the problem you are facing.

- **Come up with a range of potential fixes**: Come up with a bunch of different ideas for how to solve the problem. Don't hold back, even the wackiest ideas might spark a brilliant solution.

- **Make sure everyone involved is aware:** Teamwork makes the dream work, so make sure everyone is on the same page. Once you have selected a course of action, try to communicate it to everyone involved.

- **Think aloud**: "Two heads are better than one". And it's true! Share your ideas with others and ask them to do the same. Sometimes, talking it out can help you get new insights and breakthroughs.

- **Give ideas enough time to "gel":** Your ideas are like the ingredients in a recipe, and they need time to come together and create something delicious! So, don't rush your brainstorming process. Give your ideas time to "gel" and see how they fit together. Sometimes, the best solutions take a little time to simmer and develop.

The following diagram breaks down the whole process of problem-solving into a few simple steps. Let us understand each step in more detail, starting with analyzing the problem:

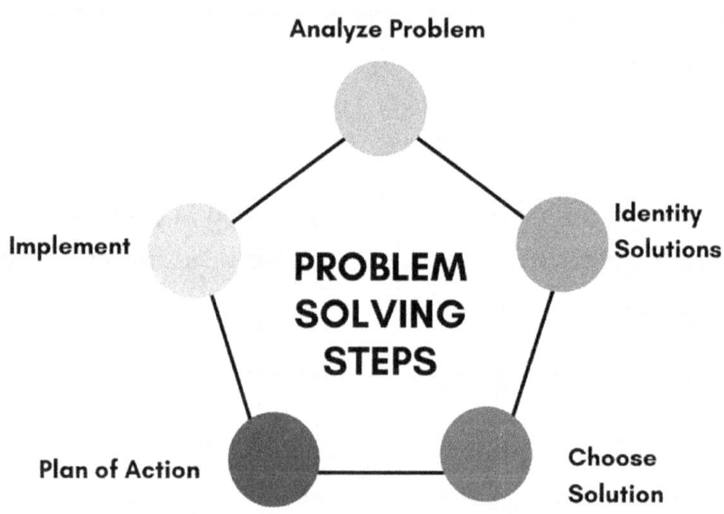

1. Analyze the problem

Before you jump straight to any conclusion and make hasty decisions, it is better to analyze the problem and look for possible courses of action. Have you ever heard the saying "Look before you leap"? Well, it applies to problem-solving, too! Before you dive headfirst into solving a problem, it is crucial to know what it is. You need to put on the detective hat and gather clues, assess the situation, and understand all the angles before you can crack the case. Why is this step so important? To build a strong foundation for your solution. When you take the time to analyze a problem, you are giving yourself a roadmap to success. You can spot potential pitfalls, come up with creative solutions, and make sure your plan is watertight. Here is how you can analyze your problems:

- **Try alternative viewpoints**: When you are analyzing a problem, it is imperative to consider different perspectives. With alternative viewpoints, you can get a deeper understanding of the problem and come up with more effective solutions.

- **Be adaptable when doing your analysis**: Problems are rarely simple; they have several dimensions, so it is imperative to stay flexible in your approach. At every point, you may discover a new angle to the story, which means that you will have to change your thought process according to the unfolding situation. So, be adaptable while analyzing the problem.

- **Take into account different impact strands:** Every problem has ripple effects, so it is crucial to think about how different factors might be interconnected. By taking into account different impact strands, you can uncover hidden connections and address the problem more effectively.

- **Research issues that you don't have all the answers to**. Sometimes, you will encounter problems where you don't have all the answers right away. That's where research comes in! By doing your background check and gathering information, you can make a more educated analysis and come up with better solutions.

2. Formulate Possible Solutions

Have you ever been in a sticky situation where your emotions are running high, and your brain feels like it is stuck in a fog? We have all been there! When the heat is on, and your emotions are in overdrive, finding a solution to a problem can feel like trying to solve a puzzle with missing pieces. But don't worry! Even when the odds seem stacked against you, there is a way out. By taking a step back, breathing deep, and summoning your inner strategist, you can steer through the chaos and find your way to a solution. You just need to be smart and strategic and follow these steps:

- **Make a list of all the choices and assess them**: After assessing the problem, write down every possible solution that pops into your head. No idea is too wild! Then, take a closer look at each option.

- **Consider the possible effects of the choices you make**: Think of your decisions as a domino chain, one move can set off a chain reaction. Before you make your next move, take a step back and think about the big picture. Take into consideration the broader impact and make decisions that not only benefit you but also those around you.

- **Try to think of all possible solutions**: Never hesitate to push your boundaries and explore uncharted territory. Sometimes, the most unexpected solutions turn out to be the most brilliant ones. So, brainstorm ideas and see where your creativity takes you!

- **Consider similar problems:** Your past experiences are a treasure trove of wisdom. Reflect on similar challenges you have faced before and how you tackled them. What strategies worked? What flopped? Learn from your past adventures to avoid repeating the same mistakes.

3. Choose a solution

The next step is to find an appropriate solution to the problem. How would you do that? Is there one single formula to crack every problem? No! You have to look into various approaches and paths and pick the one that suits your situation and your end goals. Here is how you can find a perfect solution to any of your problems. Look into all the solutions and compare them with a set standard. An effective solution has the following characteristics:

- **It is compatible with your priorities**: Your priorities are your North Star! They guide you on your journey through life. When formulating a solution to a problem, ask yourself if this solution aligns with what's most important to you. Will it help me move closer to my goals and values? By choosing solutions that match your priorities, you are setting yourself up for success and staying true to what matters most.

- **It is the least risky**: Just imagine yourself as a rope walker balancing yourself on a thin wire. Every decision you make comes with its own set of risks. When evaluating potential solutions, consider the level of risk involved. Ask yourself what are the potential consequences of this solution. How much am I willing to risk? By weighing your risks and benefits, you can make informed decisions that minimize the chance of risks and maximize your chances of success.

- **It is full of practicality:** It is your trusty sidekick, as it keeps you grounded and focused on what is achievable. When brainstorming solutions to a problem, consider how practical they are. Think about it! Is this solution realistic, given my resources and constraints? Can I realistically implement this solution? If yes, then that's the solution you should be going after.

4. Create a Plan of Action

Your solution won't work out on its own! You will have to create a feasible action plan to culminate your ideas into reality. This calls for an action plan. Have you seen one of those action movies in which the protagonists lay out a map and devise a complete plan to fight back? Creating an action plan is like that. To create this plan, you think about all the steps of action and how to implement them. For instance, if you want to get into your dream college and you don't have enough resources, the solution would be to gather the resources through savings. Your action plan, in this case, would include the exact strategy to make and save money by doing odd jobs or avoiding unnecessary expenses and setting up a timeline to execute this plan.

5. Implement- Walk the Talk

And once you reach a solution you are quite confident about, implement it right away. Be confident about your choices; even if the solution doesn't work out in your favor, you can always restart this process and devise new solutions to the problem until you achieve a successful outcome. And the results you will get will definitely be worth all the effort and time you put in. Plus, you will learn so much along the way that you will come out as a much stronger and more resilient person than ever before.

With that, we have reached the end of this chapter. I hope you have learned some invaluable lessons about the importance of choices and ways to make decisions that suit your life. We have gone through some of the decision-making challenges you might be facing in your teenage and also tried to find suitable solutions. Now, it's about time to use the different techniques of problem-solving and decision-making shared in this chapter, analyze your problems, brainstorm solutions, and then pick the approach that guarantees positive results. Remember, personal growth is a journey, so keep refining your decision-making skills along the way.

Let's Brainstorm!

Do you want to test your problem-solving capabilities? Do you want to know how you would deal with different issues and which techniques would you employ? Well, here is a quick brainstorming session for you! Imagine yourself in different scenarios given below and answer their respective questions to learn about your problem-solving skills. While thinking about the given problems, take your time and write the answers without any judgment. All the best!

Scenario # 01:

You have a major school project due next week, but your friends are inviting you on a spontaneous weekend trip. How will you prioritize your time and make a decision?

Questions:

What are the short-term and long-term consequences of neglecting your school project for the trip?

____

____

How important is academic success to you, and how does it align with your goals?

____

____

Have you considered the potential regret of missing out on the trip versus the satisfaction of completing your project?

____

____

Are there compromises you could make, such as completing some work before the trip or finding a way to work on the project during the trip?

____

____

How do your past experiences with time management and prioritization inform your decision-making process?

____

____

Scenario # 02:

You find yourself torn between pursuing a career path that your parents approve of but which lacks your passion or following your own dreams, which your parents do not fully support. How would you navigate this dilemma?

Questions:

What are the values and expectations that your parents have instilled in you regarding career choices?

____

____

How important is parental approval to you in making your career decisions?

____

____

What risks and potential rewards come with following your own dreams despite parental disapproval?

____

____

Have you considered seeking a compromise or finding common ground with your parents regarding your career aspirations?

____

____

How might your decision impact your relationship with your parents and your own sense of fulfillment?

____

____

Scenario # 03:

You are part of a group project at school, and one of your team members isn't pulling their weight. The project is due soon, and the team's grade will depend on it. How do you address the situation?

Questions:

What are the potential consequences of confronting a team member versus letting the situation continue?

How do your values regarding teamwork and fairness influence your approach to resolving the issue?

Have you considered seeking guidance from your teacher or a trusted adult about how to handle the situation?

What strategies could you employ to encourage the team member to contribute without causing conflict?

How might your decision impact the dynamics of future group projects and your own reputation among peers and teachers?

Scenario # 04:

You have been offered the opportunity to study abroad for a semester, but it means being away from your family and friends for an extended period. How do you decide whether to take this opportunity?

Questions:

What are the potential personal and academic benefits of studying abroad?

____

____

How important is staying connected with your family and friends to you, and how might you maintain those relationships while abroad?

____

____

Have you considered the cultural and experiential enrichment that studying abroad could offer?

____

____

What fears or concerns do you have about being away from home, and how might you address them?

____

____

How does this decision align with your long-term goals and aspirations?

____

____

Scenario # 05:

You witness a classmate being bullied by a group of peers, but you are unsure whether to intervene. How do you decide what action to take?

Questions:

What are the potential risks and benefits of intervening in this situation?

____

____

How do your values regarding kindness, empathy, and standing up for others influence your decision?

____

____

Have you considered the potential consequences of not taking action, both for the bullied classmate and for the overall school environment?

____

____

What strategies could you use to safely intervene or seek help from a teacher or school counselor?

____

____

How might your decision impact your own sense of moral integrity and your relationships with your peers?

____

____

CHAPTER 7

Digital Literacy and Online Safety

"Embracing innovation and understanding how to navigate the digital era is the key to unlocking new opportunities and staying ahead of the curve."

— **Nicky Verd**

ave you ever heard the phrase, "All the world's a stage"? Well, in today's world, that stage is more the internet, and we all are players on it. What do you think your role is in this digital world? Do you ever wonder if the stuff you see online is legit? Or worry about who is seeing your posts? Then, don't let your thoughts settle down! These are some really important questions to think about as you scroll through your social media feeds or surf the web. I cannot deny the fact that the internet is pretty awesome, no doubt! But it has its tricky parts, too, such as cyberbullying, online scams, data theft, fake news, etc. But guess what? You have the power to deal with these challenges and avoid the harm that comes with unthoughtful use of the internet! You can be technology and internet-savvy enough to spot fake news, protect your privacy, and stay safe from online bullies. It just requires a little understanding, a deeper realization of the long-term consequences of your online activities, and some concrete actions in the right direction to safely use the internet for your own advantage. So, let's make sure we are not just random players in this digital world but smart directors of our own online stories!

Importance of Digital Literacy

Digital literacy simply means having an understanding of the online world and knowing how to use it safely without compromising your own privacy and that of anyone else. It is not about restricting yourself but allowing yourself to use all the available online resources, platforms, and tools in a more effective manner. Once you become digitally literate, you will be able to:

Navigate the Online World: The Internet is like a massive jungle full of information. Being digitally literate equips you with a trusty map and compass. It quickly helps you find what you really need and prevents you from getting lost in the wilderness of misinformation.

Secure Yourself: Just as you look both ways before crossing the street, being digitally literate teaches you how to stay safe online. You can learn about cyberbullying, privacy settings, and how to spot sketchy websites and individuals so you can keep yourself and your friends safe.

Speak Your Mind: From sharing memes to posting on Instagram or chatting in group chats, you can enjoy all such activities when you are digitally literate. You can learn how to communicate effectively, respectfully, and with your own unique flair.

Think like Sherlock Holmes: Not everything on the internet is true. It is a shocker, I know! Digital literacy helps you become super sleuths who can identify real information from fake news. It makes you your own detective for sorting fact from fiction.

Unleash Your Creativity: The more you know about the digital world, the more you understand the productive and creative ways to make money without putting your self-respect and privacy at risk. You can learn to become a YouTuber, a vlogger, a graphic designer, or even a social media influencer. Being digitally literate unlocks a treasure trove of creative opportunities for you. You can edit videos, design graphics, and make your online presence pop!

Future-Proof Your Dreams: In today's world, being tech-savvy gives you the golden ticket to the chocolate factory of opportunities. Digital literacy sets us up for success in school, careers, and whatever adventures come our way.

Become a Changemaker: Do you want to make a difference in the world? Being digitally literate means, you can use your online powers for good. Whether it is spreading awareness, starting a petition, or fundraising for a cause, you can be superheroes from behind your screens.

Risks & Challenges of Going Online

The internet is a good source of limitless knowledge, and it provides you with platforms where you can express yourself, connect with others, and even make a difference. It is where you can find answers to almost any question you have and share your thoughts with the world. But, just like any adventure, it comes with its fair share of risks and challenges. From cyberbullying to misinformation, there are things out there that can trip you up if you are not careful. That is why it is super important to be vigilant, protect your content and your privacy, and be mindful of what you see and share online. You are living in an age where it is almost impossible to keep yourself out of the virtual world. However, it is still possible to protect yourself from its harms as you would in the real world; you just have to be familiar with the potential threats and take respective actions to deal with those problems in time.

Cyber-bullying

Most bullies love to hide behind the anonymity of the internet and torture others through their abusive words and emotional manipulation. It is no wonder that the internet has made bullying easier than ever. It gives people a sense of power and anonymity, allowing even good kids to be mean sometimes. You know, like saying things they would never say face-to-face. It is pretty messed up, right? Some people are more likely to be targeted by cyberbullies. It's unfortunate, but it is true. It could be anyone who seems introverted, different, or just feels down about themselves. But hey, that doesn't mean it's okay to accept the bullying or that you deserve it. No one deserves to be treated like that. Being cyberbullied can really mess with your head. It is not just a few mean words online, but it can make you feel alone, sad, or even scared. In some terrible cases, it even makes you question your own identity. And that is really serious! So, instead of sitting around and tolerating cyberbullying, acknowledge its harmful effects and take concrete actions to protect yourself and others around you.

What You Can Do

"If you are experiencing cyberbullying, go talk to an adult. Don't worry if people call you 'weak' or 'immature.' Those labels won't change your reality. It actually requires courage to speak out." - Juan.

Okay, so first things first! Ask yourself, "Is it bullying?" Sometimes, people say hurtful things without really meaning to. As if they don't realize how much it can hurt. But when someone's out to hurt, harass, or threaten you online, that is straight-up bullying. And that is not cool at all. Now, here's a golden rule! How you respond can either make things better or worse. So, let me tell you how you can show online bullies their place!

1. **Ignore the bully:** I know it may sound like I am asking to chicken out, but it is the wisest thing to do. By ignoring the bully, you take his/her power of playing with your mind away. It is tough to ignore, but sometimes, not giving them any attention is the best move. You see, bullies actually feed off your reaction. If you don't react, they lose their power. Pretty smart, right? You can try this trick, and you will see how they simply back off when you block and report them online. Carmen, a young college graduate, shares her insights, **"If you ever face cyberbullying, it is wise to leave the conversation. Do you really want to share a space with a person who disrespects others? No! So, block that bully and remove yourself from such a situation. I always do the same."**

2. **Resist the urge to hit back:** Now, this step can also be counted as ignoring the bully. But here I am again, emphasizing not engaging with them. I know it is tempting to fire back in anger and frustration with some snappy comeback but trust me, it is not worth your time and energy. Basically, you don't have to stoop to their level. Just leave the conversation, comment section, or group where bullies are engaging you.

3. **Be proactive:** Don't ever let them win and feed off your reaction. Block them the minute you realize they are abusing you, save all evidence of what they have done in the form of screenshots (even if you don't read it) and tell them to back off. You have every right to stand up for yourself.

4. **Boost your confidence:** The way bullies mess with your mind is to make you feel bad about yourself, and that makes you weak and vulnerable. You can get back at bullies but doing the opposite of their intentions and boosting your confidence. Focus on your strengths and what makes you awesome. Remember, all

bullies prey on people who seem weak. Don't give them that satisfaction.

5. **Tell someone:** Never hide the bully! Share your experience with everyone around you so that they can help you every step of the way. Sharing also creates an atmosphere of discouraging bullying. So, it is important to expose the bullies and warn others as well to avoid engaging with any bully.

Let's say you are forced to face a bully in an online space that you cannot leave, such as an online class message group or an online study forum. Then, the wise thing to do is to first tell someone about your bullying experience. Share the screenshots with your parents, your teachers, or someone you trust.

Texting

Texting is a breeze, right? Yeah! Even the things that you can't say to a person's face, you can say it out loud via messages. This makes texting both an easy and tricky way of communication. It is super important to tread carefully in the digital world. Why? For starters, the words you type can sometimes be misinterpreted, which can lead to unnecessary misunderstandings or hurt someone's feelings. Plus, sharing too much personal information over text can put you at risk of cyberbullying, online harassment, or even scams. And let's not forget about the harms of texting while driving! It only takes a small distraction to cause a serious accident. So, your words have power; use them wisely!

Here is how you can mindfully send a text to someone without fearing the unintended consequences.

First, think about whom you are texting. Not everyone you barely know should have access to your message inbox. Be cautious about who you give your number to. Remember, not everyone needs to have your digits. And if your parents have guidelines about who you can talk to, it is important to respect their rules. You don't want to find yourself in a tricky situation!

Next, think before you send. Texting can sometimes lead to misunderstandings because emotions and tone of voice can be hard to convey. So, before you hit send, ask yourself if your message could be misinterpreted. And remember, if you wouldn't say it in person, it is probably best not to text it.

Finally, timing is everything when it comes to texting! It is not cool to be glued to your phone when you are hanging out with friends or having dinner with your family. Set some boundaries for yourself, like turning off your phone during meals or when you are studying. And whatever you do, never text and drive. It's just not worth the risk!

Sexting

Let's talk about something that might seem quite tempting, but it always comes with some serious consequences. Yes! I am talking about sexting. You know, sending those flirty texts or steamy pics that seem harmless at first can often land you in trouble.

You must be thinking, "Everyone does it! It's no big deal. Why can't I do it?" Most teens see sexting as a way to show they are sexually active or to flirt with someone they like. It's their way of saying, "Hey, look at me, I'm cool and confident." Plus, sometimes, some teens might feel pressured to send explicit pics because they got one first. Initially, when you are with someone, sexting might seem safer than actual sex. After all, you can't get pregnant or catch an STD from it, right? But guess what? It is not as safe as you think. Once you hit that send button, you immediately lose control of the pics or texts you sent. It could end up anywhere! On someone else's desktop, phone, social media, or worse, in the wrong hands. Imagine if your private pics were shared with everyone at school. It's embarrassing and hurting, right? Those are some serious consequences that you must consider before making up your mind about sending your private pictures to someone.

In some cases, sending or receiving explicit pics, especially if you are a minor, can be considered child abuse or distributing child pornography. Some teens have even been prosecuted as sex offenders because of sexting. This is not the label you want following you around. So, before you hit send on that risky text or pic, think twice. Is it really worth the risk?

How can we avoid it?

Anna, who recently graduated high school, shares her experience. She had been chatting with someone she met on a social media platform for a while now. They seemed to have a lot in common, and Anna enjoyed their conversations. However, one day, the person she had been talking to suddenly started sending her explicit messages and asked her to send nude photos. Now, what options were there for her?

Option A: "I don't want to upset this person, so I will just go along with it and send the photos."

Option B: "I feel really uncomfortable with this request. I'm going to tell this person that I'm not okay with sending nude photos and see how he reacts."

Option C: "This behavior is a red flag. I'm going to block and report this person for inappropriate conduct."

Anna knew that her safety was her priority, and sending any explicit picture to someone she talks online was a big risk. She thought that **Option B or C** were the most advisable choices in that scenario. So, she asserted her boundaries and took action to protect herself. She was able to maintain her integrity and self-respect in the face of inappropriate behavior.

If you have ever been in a similar situation or are simply struggling to resist the urge to sext, don't be afraid to reach out for support. Talk to a friend you can trust, a family member, or a counselor who can provide guidance and encouragement. I know sexting seems tempting in the heat of the moment, but trust me, once you fight the urge, you will thank yourself later. Here's how you can resist it:

- **Think Thrice Before You Act**

Before hitting send on that risky text or pic, take a breath and some time to think about the consequences. Ask yourself, what if the person I am sending my pictures to shares them with his or her friends, or someone hacks into their cellphone and steals your pictures for the wrong purposes? Your reputation is at stake here! So, think hard before hitting send.

- **Set Boundaries**

Even if you flirt with someone over a text, you can establish clear boundaries for yourself. Decide ahead of time what you are comfortable with and stick to it. Remember, it is okay to say no if you think sharing private pictures is wrong. Don't yield to the pressure! Think about yourself and your future only.

- **Communicate Openly**

If someone pressures you to sext, don't be afraid to speak up. Let them know that you are not okay with it and that you expect them to respect your boundaries. Real friends always try to understand and respect your decision. Remember, those who really care about you will never force you to do things that could potentially jeopardize your reputation.

- **Focus on Real Connections**

Instead of seeking validation through sexting, focus on building real connections with people who value and respect you for who you are.

True intimacy isn't about exchanging explicit pics; it is more about trust, respect, and genuine connection.

- **Find Healthy Outlets**

If you are feeling tempted to sext out of boredom or curiosity, find healthier ways to occupy your time and energy. Pick up a hobby, hang out with friends, or engage in activities that make you feel good about yourself.

Photo sharing and permission

"I keep my social media accounts 'Private' so that not just anyone could follow me. I only allow those people to follow me who I know and trust well in real life."

–Sophia.

Sharing photos online is fun and convenient. It is a great way to stay connected with friends and family, especially those who live far away. But here's the thing, if those photos are shared publicly without any privacy, they can attract all sorts of scammers and exploiters. Posting photos online can actually put your safety at risk. Some photos have geotagging, which means they reveal your exact location, and through them, you would be handing over a roadmap of your place to potential burglars. Scary, right?

But fear not; there are ways to protect yourself. First off, be picky about who you follow and what you post. If someone's content doesn't sit right with you, hit that unfollow button. And don't be afraid to set limits on your browsing time. Remember, you just need to develop better control over the content you post.

Think of your private information as the stuff you keep in your house. Would you leave your front gate open and let anyone walk in to go through your stuff, pick anything they like, and walk away? No! It would feel like getting robbed in broad daylight. The same happens with your personal content when you share it publicly. In this case, you just can't see the bulgur stealing your photos without your permission. This anonymity may give you the illusion of safety, but none of the content remains safe in the hands of people you don't even know. So, think twice before sharing and use the "privacy settings" on all the social media platforms to only give access to people you can trust in real life as well. Elain, a high schooler, shared her process by saying:

"My mother has taught me well to ask three simple questions to myself before posting stuff online:

1. **Is this picture too personal?**

2. **Could it offend people in some way?**

3. **Will I later regret having posted this photo?**

If the answer to any of those questions is yes, then it is probably wise not to share that picture online."

So, next time you are tempted to share that perfect selfie or beach pic, pause for a moment and think about the risks. With a little caution and common sense, you can enjoy the benefits of online photo sharing without putting yourself in harm's way.

Social Media

Social media is a wild horse; if you don't rein it in, it will take complete control of you. You know those times when you are just scrolling through your feed, and suddenly, hours have flown by? That is, social media draws you in and makes you waste precious time in your life.

The thing is, social media is designed to be addictive as if that is in its DNA - the algorithm to keep you spellbound for hours. The more time you spend on it, the more money advertisers make. So, ask yourself, are you losing track of time when you are scrolling? Could some of that time be better spent doing something more productive?

What you can do is set time limits for yourself. Decide how much time you will spend each day on social media and stick to it. Start by gradually decreasing your screen time and deduct fifteen minute each day. Trust me, setting boundaries will help you take back control of your time.

Social media & your sleep

It's not just the time that social media affects; it also impacts your sleep. You know you are supposed to get around eight hours a night, but how many of you actually do? And be honest, how many of you check your phone before bed and end up scrolling for hours? Not getting enough sleep messes with your mood and can lead to serious mental health conditions. Are you sacrificing sleep for social media? If so, you can end that now! How? Keep your phone out of your bedroom or turn it to silent mode at night. Seriously, it works! Using this method, try to stop using screens at least two hours before bedtime and let your brain unwind.

Social media affecting your emotions

Do you ever feel a bit down after scrolling through your feed? You are not alone. Social media can mess with your head, making you compare yourself to others and feel like you are missing out on all the fun. But the truth is, social media can't replace real human connection. Nothing you see online shows the complete picture of reality. You only see a part of it that is doctored only for social media posts. It might help you keep in touch with friends, but it is no substitute for face-to-face conversations and meaningful connections.

The power is totally in your hands! You can take a break from social media and make it stop from messing with your head. Try it out for a few days or even a week. Have you heard of the term "digital detox?" It is a proven technique to detoxify your mind from the effects of digital devices by staying away from them. During this time, you can spend more time with family and friends in person. You might be surprised at how much happier and less stressed you feel.

"I occasionally take breaks from social media by temporarily uninstalling the app. This practice helps me maintain a healthy balance in my life and concentrate on my priorities. I find there are far more fulfilling ways to spend my time than endlessly scrolling through my phone." —Jane.

So, to sum it up, social media isn't all sunshine and rainbows. With a little awareness and some healthy habits, you can make sure it is not running your life. Take control and care for your mind and your body, for they are your great resources!

My parents do not let me use social media. What should I do?

Most teens find this question relatable, and the more their parents stop them from using mobile phones or social media, the more urge they feel to use it. What do you do if your parents are adamant about not letting you use social media? It might feel like everyone around you is constantly scrolling through their feeds, and you are missing out on all the fun. But here is the thing! Many parents have good reasons for not allowing the use of social media. It is important to understand why your parents might be saying no. They are probably aware of the potential risks associated with social media, like depression, exposure to inappropriate content, and unnecessary drama with friends. And you know what? Some teens have actually chosen to ditch social media on their own because they found it was doing them more harm than good. Take Mia, for example. She realized it was eating up her time that could be better spent elsewhere. Or Jeremy, who felt like he had no control over the stuff popping up on his feed. And then there's Bethany, who found herself too caught up in what everyone else was doing.

So, the best thing to do when your parents don't budge is to cooperate with their rules. Show them that you are mature enough to respect their decisions without throwing a tantrum. Trust me, trying to sneak around or setting up a secret account will only make things worse if they find out. Plus, it is not worth the anxiety and guilt. Remember, it is important to be honest in all things.

The most empowering move is to make it your decision. Take a step back and think about whether social media is really the best choice for you right now. If you genuinely believe it is not, then own that decision. When your friends ask why you are not on social media, don't be embarrassed. Just tell them it's not your thing right now and that you are enjoying the freedom that comes with it.

Hoax of Online Popularity

Did you ever had that feeling when you see your friends racking up likes and followers, and you start to wonder if you are missing out? That is the hoax of popularity! Due to the apparent perks of being famous, every teen often feels like missing out on something if they are not popular. But, remember, fame always comes with a price. It disrupts your freedom, your peace of mind and allows people to undermine your privacy.

Sure, having a good reputation online is important. But when that desire for acceptance turns into a craving for popularity, things can get dicey. Just ask Harper, who has seen people do some crazy stuff just to get noticed. From risky stunts to downright dangerous challenges like eating laundry detergent pods, some will go to extremes for a shot at online fame.

Popularity online isn't always what it seems. Have you heard of the "humble brag"? It is when people post highlight after highlight of their seemingly perfect life, creating an illusion of popularity. But behind the scenes, it is often just smoke and mirrors. So, before you start staging photos or tagging locations you have never been to, ask yourself, is it worth compromising your beliefs and principles for a few extra likes? Instead of chasing after likes and followers, focus on being true to yourself. Post content that reflects who you are and what you stand for, not what you think will make you popular. After all, real friends will like you for who you are, not for your online persona.

Online Threats and Cybersecurity

Cybersecurity is your digital shield; the stronger the shield, the more protected you will feel against all the nasty stuff lurking on the internet. From viruses and malware to hackers and phishing scams, security systems help keep your devices and personal info safe from harm.

Online Threats to Watch Out For: The Internet is an open space, and it is shared by all sorts of cyber criminals. That is why there are a variety of threats that you should protect yourself against. Otherwise, you can lose your valuable information.

Malware or Viruses: These are malicious software programs designed to infect your devices and wreak havoc. They can steal your personal info, damage your files or even take control of your device without you knowing.

Phishing Scams: Phishing scams are sneaky efforts by hackers to trick you into giving away your personal info. They often come in the form of emails or texts that look legitimate but are actually designed to steal your personal information, passwords, and credit card numbers.

Social Engineering: This is when hackers use manipulation and deception to trick you into revealing confidential information or carrying out actions that compromise your security. They might pretend to be someone you know or trust, like a friend or family member, to gain access to your accounts.

Identity Theft: This occurs when a hacker steals your personal information, like your name, address, or social security number, and commits fraud or other crimes using that information. It can affect your finances and harm your reputation if not caught early.

If you are smart and wise about it, you can definitely avoid those sneaky attempts and show cybercriminals the door. Here are some important measures that you need to take to protect your digital devices and your information online:

Avoid Suspicious Websites and Downloads

Do you know those sketchy websites that promise free stuff or ask for your personal information? Simply steer clear of those. Stick to trusted and secure websites and app stores when downloading apps or software. If something seems too good to be true, it probably is. So, don't use any such websites.

Recognize and Avoid Phishing Scams

Have you ever gotten an email or text asking for your password or personal info? That is probably a phishing scam. Hackers use these sneaky tactics to steal your info and wreak havoc. So, if you get a suspicious message asking for sensitive information, don't click on any links or provide any personal details. Delete it ASAP. Or simply keep your "spam" option active so emails coming from suspicious accounts automatically goes to the spam folder.

Use Public Wi-Fi with Caution

Public Wi-Fi often seems convenient, but it can also be a hotbed for hackers. So, whenever you are using public Wi-Fi, avoid using or sharing your sensitive information, like your bank account or social media. If you need to use public Wi-Fi, connect to a virtual private network (VPN) first to encrypt your connection and protect your data.

Protect Your Devices

Your smartphone and laptop are like treasure chests of your personal info, so it is important to keep them secure. Make sure your devices are always password protected, and consider using biometric security features like fingerprint or face recognition. Keep your software up to date with the latest security patches and install reputable antivirus software to protect against malware.

Protect Your Personal Information

Your personal info is like gold to hackers, so guard it as if your life depends on it. Be careful about the things you share online, especially on social media. Keep your privacy high and think twice before posting sensitive info like your address or phone number.

Use Strong Passwords

Choose passwords that are hard to guess, and use a different password for each of your accounts. Here are some tips to create strong passwords that are tough to crack:

- **Use a Mix of Characters**: A strong password must include a mix of letters (both uppercase and lowercase), numbers, and special characters (! @, #, $, %). Mixing it up like this makes your password much harder for hackers to guess. For example, instead of using a simple word like **"mypassword,"** try something like **"myP@ssw0rd!".**

- **Make it Long**: The longer your password, the stronger it is. Aim for at least 12 characters or more to make it tough for hackers to crack. Instead of using a short password like "sunshine," go for something longer like "Suns#ine1234!". (Make sure to keep it saved somewhere).

- **Avoid Common Words or Phrases**: Hackers can easily guess passwords that are based on common phrases or words. Stay away from things like "123456," "password," or your name. Instead of using your pet's name like "fluffy123," mix it up with numbers and special characters like "Flu$fy789!".

- **Don't Use Personal Info**: Avoid using easily accessible information like your birthday, address or phone number in your passwords. Hackers can easily find this info and use it against you. Instead of using your birthdate like "05132005," go for something unrelated like "B1rthd@y0520!".

- **Change it Up:** Don't use the same password for all your accounts. If a hacker cracks one of your passwords, they will gain access to all your accounts. Mix it up and use different passwords for each account. Instead of using the same password for your email, social media, and banking accounts, create unique passwords for each one, like "Em@ilP@ss123," "Soc!@lMe#ia456," and "B@nkSecr$t789!".

Report Cyber Threats

If you come across cybercrime or any suspicious activity or behavior online, report it to the appropriate authorities or organizations. This helps protect not only yourself but also others who might be targeted by the same threats. Search for cybercrime authorities in your country and then report the crime directly to them.

Using Technology Wisely

Sure, smartphones, computers, and video games are awesome, but like anything else, too much of a good thing can be, well, not so good. Follow these tips to make sure you are using technology in a way that is both smart and balanced:

Assess Your Use of Technology:

Take a moment to think about how much time you spend on your devices and how it affects your life. Do you feel anxious when you are not online? Are you missing out on sleep or neglecting other important things like spending time with family or getting schoolwork done? If so, it might be time to make some changes.

Identify what your technology needs and your wants are. Using the internet to study and make an assignment is a need, but playing Tekken on your PlayStation for hours is simply a desire that may consume your precious time and energy without giving you any productive results. After identifying your technology needs, try to focus on them and avoid paying heed to the outside noises.

Set Reasonable Limits

Just like you set limits on how much junk food you eat or how late you stay out with friends, it is super important to set limits on your screen time, too. Choose a time limit to spend on your devices each day and stick to it. And if you need a little help sticking to your limits, ask a family member or friend to help keep you accountable.

Avoid the Digital Trap

It is easy to get sucked into the digital world, but remember, there is a whole lot more to life than what is on your screen. Make sure you are not missing out on real-life experiences, like hanging out with friends, playing sports, or enjoying the great outdoors. Balance is key!

Don't Let Technology Control You

Technology is awesome, but it should never control your life. If you find yourself feeling like you can't live without your phone or computer, it might be time to take a step back and reevaluate your priorities. Remember, you are in control, not your devices.

Make the Best Use of Your Time

Time is precious, so make sure you are using it wisely. Instead of mindlessly scrolling through social media or playing video games for hours, find actual physical activities that enrich your life and bring you joy. Whether it is trying a new hobby, spending time with loved ones, or volunteering in your community, there are plenty of ways to make the most of your time.

Digital Skills That Come in Handy

Technology is not all that bad; if you learn to use it right, you can even turn it to your advantage. In fact, there are a lot of digital skills that you can easily learn through online and offline courses. Learning these skills will not only help you become technology savvy but also help you make a living from them. The advancement in technology is rapidly causing a shift in the job market, and today, you can start making some good money by learning and using some of the highly paid digital skills, such as:

Digital or Social Media Marketing

Have you ever wondered how those cool brands and influencers get so many followers and likes? This is where social media marketing comes in. Platforms like Instagram, TikTok, and Snapchat are used to promote services and products, spread brand awareness, and interact with followers. Learning the methods and techniques of social media marketing, like running an ad campaign and setting up social media profiles, etc., can give you a leg up in the job market and even help you build your own personal brand online. If you really love the idea, then you can take an online course during your summer break or even enroll for a digital marketing diploma after high school.

Search Engine Marketing (SEM)

Have you ever wondered how Google always knows exactly what you are looking for? This is where search engine optimization, or its marketing, plays a part. It is used for paid advertising to increase visibility on search engine results pages. You can learn the basics of SEM and offer your expertise to various clients to boost their website traffic, increase brand awareness, and reach target customers exactly when they are searching for products or services.

Video Creation

In case you haven't noticed, video making is a big deal these days. From YouTube to TikTok to Instagram Reels, video content is the game of the day. By learning how to compose compelling videos, you can create content that stands out in a vastly crowded digital world, whether you are promoting a business, sharing someone's talents, or just having fun online. Plus, it is a super valuable skill to have in today's visual-centric world.

Coding

This skill might sound a bit intimidating, but trust me, it is worth it, and the future has great scope for coders. Learning how to code opens up a whole world of opportunities, from building websites and apps to automating tasks and analyzing data. Plus, it teaches you valuable problem-solving skills and helps you think critically about technology. Whether you are interested in software development or data science or just want to understand how computers work, coding is an essential skill for the digital age.

These days, there are lots of online platforms where you can search for digital skills courses and learn them even for free. Let me list a few platforms to get you started:

- Coursera: https://www.coursera.org/
- edX: https://www.edx.org/
- Udemy: https://www.udemy.com/
- Khan Academy: https://www.khanacademy.org/
- Codecademy: https://www.codecademy.com/
- Treehouse: https://teamtreehouse.com/
- LinkedIn Learning (formerly Lynda.com): https://www.linkedin.com/learning/
- Skillshare: https://www.skillshare.com/
- Pluralsight: https://www.pluralsight.com/
- Google Digital Garage: https://learndigital.withgoogle.com/digitalgarage
- FutureLearn: https://www.futurelearn.com/
- Udacity: https://www.udacity.com/
- Skillcrush: https://skillcrush.com/
- FreeCodeCamp: https://www.freecodecamp.org/
- The Odin Project: https://www.theodinproject.com/

Once you learn these skills, you can use online freelancing platforms to sell your services anywhere in the world. You can read their respective guidelines, create a seller's account, list your services, and start selling. Here are some platforms that you can try:

- Upwork: https://www.upwork.com/
- Freelancer: https://www.freelancer.com/
- Fiverr: https://www.fiverr.com/
- Toptal: https://www.toptal.com/
- Guru: https://www.guru.com/
- PeoplePerHour: https://www.peopleperhour.com/
- SimplyHired: https://www.simplyhired.com/
- FlexJobs: https://www.flexjobs.com/

So, what are you waiting for? Get out there and start learning!

"The future belongs to those who learn more skills and combine them in creative ways."

- Robert Greene

With this great quote, I would like to bring this chapter to an end. Here, we have learned the art of becoming a literate and responsible digital citizen. The ways to protect your online presence and deal with cyberbullying and cyber threats are thoroughly discussed. Social media and the internet are the most creative ways to connect with others and share knowledge and information with others, but when used without precaution, the perks of these tools can turn into perils quickly. This is why it is high time that we all understand the importance of being wise and smart about internet usage and do not let technology control us.

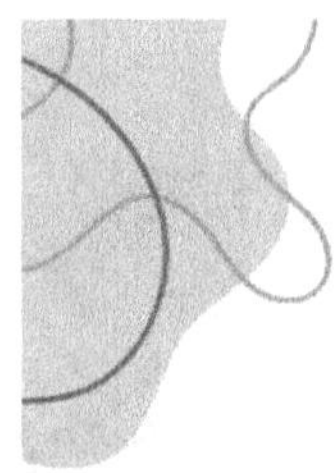

THE MINDFUL BYTES

- How much time do you spend online each day, and how does it affect your daily life?

- What are your favorite online activities, and do they contribute positively to your well-being?

- Are there any negative consequences of excessive internet use that you've noticed in your life or the lives of your friends?

- Have you ever witnessed or experienced cyberbullying? How did it make you feel?

- What steps can you take to prevent cyberbullying, both as a victim and as a bystander?

- What precautions do you take to protect your personal information and devices online?

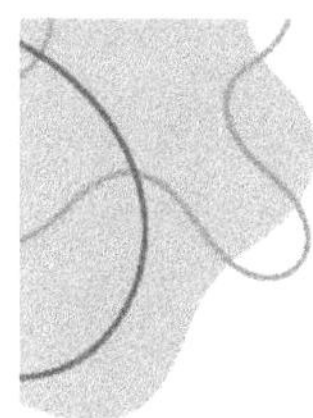

THE MINDFUL BYTES

- Do you use strong, unique passwords for your online accounts, or do you tend to reuse usernames?

  ____

  ____

- How can you support friends who may be experiencing cyberbullying?

  ____

  ____

- Are you aware of common cyberthreats, such as phishing scams, malware, and identity theft?

  ____

  ____

- How can you distinguish between legitimate online sources and potential cyberthreats?

  ____

  ____

- Are there any negative effects of social media usage that you've observed in yourself or your peers?

  ____

  ____

- How can you use technology and social media platforms responsibly and in a way that aligns with your values?

  ____

  ____

CHAPTER 8

Emotional Resilience, Stress Management and Emotional Well-being

"What lies behind us and what lies before us are tiny matters compared to what lies within us."

— **Ralph Waldo Emerson**

On February 13, 2023, CDC - the Centers for Disease Control and Prevention gave out a report on the mental health of teenagers in the United States. In this report, they highlighted that over 40 percent of high school students suffer from persistent sadness and hopelessness. And it is quite true that the teenage era is one of the most stressful stages of your life. A lot changes when you become a teen. Life can throw all sorts of stress your way, from high school pressures to social anxieties and everything in between. How do you manage your emotional highs and lows? What stress factors weigh the heaviest on your mind? If you struggle with emotional and mental challenges, then it's time to realize their potential harm and learn different coping mechanisms to counter all the triggering factors. Right now, it is super important to recognize that it is okay to feel overwhelmed at times. The stress management techniques, emotional regulation practices, and methods of emotional resilience shared in this chapter can serve as invaluable tools for you to navigate all the challenges of life.

The Power of Emotional Intelligence and Resilience

Do you know what is so amazing and beautiful about human existence? It is the entire range of emotions we can feel and express. Our emotions differentiate us from the rest of the living beings, and these emotions can both be our friends and enemies. When emotions are not understood and regulated, they can disrupt our lives and progress, whereas when we become someone who is more attuned to their own feelings, then we develop the power to even conquer the world. This superpower of comprehending, controlling, and using emotions in the right way is collectively called emotional intelligence. And once you become capable of keeping your emotions in check, in different circumstances, you become emotionally resilient. There are several advantages of taking the reign of your emotions into your own hands. With emotional resilience, you learn to bounce back from all the setbacks, stay composed under pressure, and build stronger relationships through effective communication and empathy. This resilience empowers you to pursue your dreams with determination and overcome obstacles along the way. Plus, emotional well-being also protects your mental health and helps you recognize and manage your emotions, cope with stress healthily, and seek support when needed. You will only find real happiness and positivity in your life when you embrace who you truly are and appreciate the little things every day.

How do I Know If I am Stressed?

Sometimes, we underestimate stress. We believe that only if we distract ourselves with video games or other mind-occupying activities can we make this unknown feeling of stress and anxiety go away. But the thing about suppressed emotions is that they mess with your mind and resurface in the form of frustration, anger, and bad behavior. So, the best way to deal with stress is to first recognize the symptoms, process your emotions, and find the causes behind them so that you can take concrete and effective actions. Here are some symptoms of stress and depression that you should watch out for:

- **Feeling nervous or anxious**: If you are constantly feeling on edge or worrying excessively about things, it could be a sign of stress or anxiety.

- **Frequently feeling tired**: Stress can take a toll on your energy levels, which often leaves you feeling tired even after a full night's sleep.

- **Stomach aches and chest pain**: Stress can manifest physically and lead to symptoms of stomach aches or chest pain. If you are experiencing unexplained physical symptoms, it might be linked to stress.

- **Procrastinating or neglecting responsibilities**: Trouble focusing or getting things done can also be a sign of stress overwhelming you. It makes you put off tasks or neglect your responsibilities.

- **Feeling overwhelmed:** If you are feeling like everything is too much to handle or you are struggling to cope with daily life, it could be a sign of stress overload.

- **Moodiness:** Stress and depression can mess with your mood and make you feel super sad, irritated, or have mood swings that don't match what's going on around you.

If any of those symptoms ever occur to you or anyone you know, then it is a clear indication that you need to take immediate measures to counter your stress.

What's Making Me Stressful?

Before looking into various stress management techniques, let us first address the causes so that you can take targeted actions to avoid or contain the situations that put you in distress. Here are some common sources of stress you could face as a teen:

- **Expectations and annoyances from school:** Whether it is the pressure to excel academically, dealing with strict teachers, or feeling overwhelmed by homework and exams, school can be a major source of stress.

- **Negative ideas or emotions about yourself**: Self-esteem and body image issues are real at this age. It can make you feel stressed and anxious. Sophie Turner, a widely known actress, bravely opened up about her struggles with depression and the effects of negative social media commentary. In a discussion on Dr. Phil's podcast series, she revealed that negative feedback on social media had deeply affected her, especially during her teenage years. Turner shared that comments about her weight and skin during puberty took a toll on her self-esteem, and that made her feel worthless. At one point, Turner admitted to having a difficult time getting out of bed and even contemplating suicide. However, she found solace in therapy, which played a pivotal role in her journey toward healing and self-acceptance. Turner's story shows how important mental health care is and why we need to be kind and supportive, both online and in real life.

- **Alterations to the body**: Puberty brings about physical changes that can be both exciting and stressful as you navigate new experiences and feelings about your body.

- **Issues involving friends**: Peer pressure, conflicts with friends, and bullying are common stressors for teens, especially when you try to fit in and establish your social identity.

- **Unsafe neighbourhood or living conditions:** Living in an environment where safety is a concern can create ongoing stress and tension for you and your family.

- **Parental divorce or separation**: Family dynamics can undergo significant changes during adolescence, and dealing with divorce or separation can be an added emotional challenge for teens who experience such situations. This stress factor is not common for all, and if you are not going through it, then it is definitely a blessing.

- **Prolonged sickness or serious issues within the family:** Coping with illness or other family problems can be incredibly stressful for teens, especially if it disrupts your daily routine or requires you to take on additional responsibilities.

- **Uncertainty about the future and fear of change**: The transition from teenage to adulthood brings about many uncertainties, including decisions about education, future career paths, and relationships. This extreme ambiguity about the future can lead to feelings of stress and anxiety.

Behaviors to Decrease Stress

Remember, our mental well-being is just as important as our physical health. However, we often overlook most of our emotional and mental issues as if they are not going to affect our lives. The only difference between physical and mental health is that you can see a broken limb, but you can't always see a broken mind. Just like you would go to the doctor if you had a broken limb, it is important to get your mental issues diagnosed by seeking help from a counselor or therapist and following practices that could keep the brain healthy. Just like you would do pushups to make your muscles strong, you need to adopt some behavioral changes to counter the stress and keep the mind fit. Here are some basic behavioral changes to get you started with stress management:

Learn to Say No: Saying no to tasks and commitments is something that we have already gone through in the chapter about "time management." Here, at the expense of sounding redundant, I am highlighting it again but with an entirely different context. You need to say "no" to avoid stress! Do you feel overwhelmed with too many commitments? Then, it is okay to set boundaries and say no when you are stretched too thin. You have your limitations, and recognizing them is a sign of strength, not weakness. Saying no doesn't mean you are letting anyone down; it means you are taking care of yourself and making sure that you have the capacity to handle what is on your plate. If turning someone down feels tough, buy yourself some time by saying, "Let me get back to you." Take a moment to assess whether you genuinely have the time and energy to take on the additional task or commitment.

Speaking to Yale students in 2015, Lady Gaga mentioned how she started saying "no" for her own well-being. She said:

"I started to say no. I'm not doing that. I don't want to do that. I'm not taking that picture, I'm not going to that event, I'm not standing

by that because that's not what I stand for. Slowly but surely, I remembered who I was. And then you go home, and you look in the mirror, and you are like, 'Yes. I can go to bed with you every night.' Because that person, I know that person."

Deal with Procrastination: We know that when we feel overwhelmed, we tend to procrastinate and delay doing the tasks at hand. But it only creates more stress and tension. So, it is best to fight your procrastination and get the work done in due time. If the task seems too daunting, then use the same "chunking" technique we discussed earlier in the book to break large tasks into smaller ones and work on them one at a time. You will find it easier to continue making progress.

Cut Out the Clutter: A messy room can make you feel stressed and overwhelmed. Use the methods we studied in the chapter on "organizational skills," and try to spend a few minutes tidying up your space before bed to make your mornings smoother and less chaotic. Clearing physical clutter can help clear mental clutter, making it easier to focus and stay relaxed. As Mary Johanson once said, *"Clutter is a weight that has built on top of you so gradually, you don't even realize anymore that it is holding you down."* So, the moment you get rid of the clutter, you will feel lighter than ever before.

Stop Comparing Yourself with Others: Constant comparison is a direct result of looking at people's social media feeds all the time. When you see them sharing only the good side of their lives, you are forced to think less of yourself. You feel like you are not good enough. But you must remember that everyone's journey is different, and you are doing the best you can with what you have. You just need to focus on your own progress and achievements and celebrate your unique strengths and talents without comparing yourself with others.

Look at the Big Picture: When you are feeling stressed about something, take a step back and look at the big picture. Will this matter a week from now? A month from now? A year from now? Putting things into perspective can help you realize that some things are not worth stressing over.

Planning Beforehand: Timely planning can help you avoid last-minute stress. Instead of leaving every task for the eleventh hour, create a schedule to stay on track. By making careful planning, you can manage your time more effectively and reduce the pressure and stress of looming deadlines.

Take Care of Your Body: Your mind and your body are both intertwined together. What you think affects your body, and what you eat affects your mind as well. Take care of your body by eating healthy, working out regularly, and getting enough sleep to keep your mind strong and healthy. Develop a fixed and consistent sleep schedule and a calming bedtime routine to unwind and prepare for a restful night's sleep.

Adele, one of the most sensational singers of our time, shared her experience of coping with anxiety through exercise and losing weight. In an interview, she said:

"I realized that when I was working out, I didn't have any anxiety. It was never about losing weight. I thought, If I can make my body physically strong and I can feel that and see that, then maybe one day I can make my emotions and my mind physically strong."

Connect with Others: Sharing your feelings helps you cope with them. Keeping everything inside can cause more distress. That is why you shouldn't hesitate to talk to your family, friends, or trusted adults for support when you are feeling stressed. When you share your struggles with them, they can offer emotional support to alleviate your feelings of isolation. Remember, you don't have to go through tough times alone.

Relaxing Exercises

There are times when life can feel like it is piling on pressure, but here is the good news! There are tons of exercises and techniques you can try every day to keep stress away. Whether you are into deep breathing exercises, taking a stroll in nature, jotting down your thoughts, or just chilling out and disconnecting for a bit, there is a bunch of cool stuff you can try out to feel better.

Deep Breathing

This exercise is like a chill pill for your mind. Focus on making your breaths slow and steady, allowing your body to relax with each breath.

- Get comfy in a quiet spot where you can comfortably exercise without getting distracted.

- Shut your eyes and take a deep breath, and in your head, count from 1-4.

- Now, hold your breath and repeat the counting.

- Slowly exhale through your mouth and again count from 1-4 in your head.

- Keep doing that deep breathing thing for a few minutes, and really focus on making each breath nice and slow.

Progressive Muscle Relaxation (PMR)

In this exercise, you progressively tense and relax your body muscles to induce relaxation. It trains the mind to keep control of the muscles even in tense situations.

- First, try clenching your toes and feet super tight for about 5-10 seconds.

- Release the built-up tension, and then let your muscles relax completely for 15-20 seconds.

- Move on to the next muscle group, such as your calves and thighs, and repeat the process of tensing and relaxing.

- Keep going, tense up different muscle groups in your body, like your legs, your stomach, and your arms, until you reach your head and neck.

- Take your time with each muscle group and pay attention to the sensations of tension and relaxation.

Mindfulness Meditation

"Now I meditate twice a day for half an hour. In meditation, I can let go of everything. I'm not Hugh Jackman. I'm not a dad. I'm not a husband. I'm just dipping into that powerful source that creates everything. I take a little bath in it."

- Hugh Jackman.

Sometimes, mere behavioral changes do not work to counter stress. Sure, they are necessary to manage stressful situations and make things easier for you, but additional support and help are required to relax the mind when it goes into the "fight and flight system." It is our body's natural mechanism to respond to threats, problems, and harmful situations. When this system activates, our muscles tense up, our eyes dilate, and our heartbeat accelerates. When you are constantly triggered by stressful situations, the body learns to remain in this tense mode and doesn't regain its relaxed state. This leads to further health complications in the long run. That is why it is necessary to calm the mind and deactivate the fight-and-flight system to relax a bit.

Fortunately, there are certain exercises that you can try regularly. Mindfulness is one of the highly prescribed techniques that all psychologists suggest for countering stress. Picture yourself totally in the zone, playing your favourite video game. When you are really into it, you are fully into what is happening on the screen, right? That is mindfulness! It gives your brain a power-up so you can concentrate better, feel calmer, and handle whatever life throws at you. So, how do you do it? There are various methods to carry out this practice. Let's discover them all.

Breathing Exercise

You can spend a few minutes each day practicing mindful breathing exercises. It instantly relaxes your mind and calms your brain. To do this, follow these simple steps:

- First, get yourself seated in a comfortable position and close your eyes. Sitting in a calm and noise-free environment works best for this exercise.

- Pay attention to your breath as you breathe in and out. Feel how it feels without trying to change how you breathe.

- When your mind wanders, slowly bring your focus back to your breath without feeling bad about it.

- Just notice any thoughts, feelings, or stuff popping up, and let them come and go without getting all tangled up in them.

- Continue doing this exercise for 3-5 minutes each day, then slowly and carefully increase the duration as you become more comfortable doing it.

Visualization

Take a mental vacation by imagining yourself in a peaceful and calming environment, like a sunny beach in Thailand or a quiet forest in the Alps. Picture in your mind all the cool stuff you would see, hear, and feel in this super chill place to help your mind chill out and relax.

- Close your eyes and imagine a peaceful and calming place you like or a place that you have visited before.

- Think about all the details of that place, like the colors of the visuals, the smell of the grass, the chirping of the birds, the sound of the water flowing, etc.

- Get yourself totally immersed in the visualization and take deep breaths to relax and unwind.

- Spend a few minutes in this serene mental space. Enjoy the feelings of peace and tranquility.

Engage in Relaxing Activities

You don't always have to be a monk to relax your mind. Sometimes, doing simple activities that you normally enjoy can relax your mind. If you find listening to music relaxing, then do it. It can be any activity of your choice, such as drawing or coloring, reading a book, taking a warm bath, or going for a leisurely walk outdoors. Find what brings you joy and make time for it regularly.

Yoga and Stretching

Yoga poses, or stretching exercises, are another way to relieve tension in your body and induce relaxation. Focus on deep breathing and mindful movement as you flow through different poses or stretches.

- Find gentle yoga poses or stretching exercises on YouTube.

- Follow the suggested steps to practice those poses mindfully, and pay attention to your breath and the sensations in your body.

- Move slowly and gently into each pose and avoid any of those movements that could cause pain or discomfort.

- Hold each pose for a few breaths, relax, and release tension.

Journaling

Writing down your thoughts and feelings in a journal is a great way to process your emotions and relieve stress. Journaling is a legit stress-releasing technique that experts suggest to help you gain clarity, express yourself creatively, and reflect on your experiences.

- Set aside some time each day to write in a journal, either in the morning or evening.

- Let your thoughts, feelings, and experiences flow, and write them down without judgment. Express whatever comes to mind.

- You can always read and reflect on your entries every now and then to gain insights into your thoughts and feelings, as well as to track your progress over time.

Guided Relaxation Apps or Videos

Often, it is hard to focus on a single thought when you meditate all by yourself. For those who find it difficult to focus, guided relaxation tools are the best shot. You can explore guided relaxation apps or videos online that are specifically designed for teens to help them focus. These resources can give you guidance and support as you learn to relax.

- Search for various guided relaxation apps or videos online and select the ones that have the best reviews.

- From the selected apps, choose a guided meditation, breathing exercise, or relaxation technique that appeals to you.

- Follow along with audio or video instructions, then allow yourself to relax and unwind as you listen.

- Use these resources regularly as part of your relaxation routine. You can always experiment with different guided practices to find what works best for you.

Dealing with Emotions and Building Resilience

Do you ever feel like your emotions are all over the place, kind of like riding a rollercoaster with sudden twists and turns? You are not alone in this, my friend! The ups and downs of teenage years can make it seem like your emotions are out of control, but there are things you can do to manage them wisely. The journey through adolescence is filled with hormonal changes, social pressures, academic stress, and newfound responsibilities, all of which can raise the intensity of your emotions. With a little time, a lot of patience, and constant practice, you can learn to understand and manage your emotions more effectively. Let's find out how!

1. **Identify Your Emotions**: The first step for regulating your emotions is to recognize what you are feeling. There are always deeper emotions connected to our superficial feelings. Take some time to check in with yourself throughout the day and pay attention to how you are feeling. Are you feeling happy, sad, angry, anxious, or something else? Sometimes, emotions can be complex and mixed, so try to pinpoint exactly what you are experiencing.

2. **Label Your Emotions**: Once you have identified your emotions, try to put them into words. Use specific terms to label your emotions as "frustrated or angry," "envious or jealous," "happy or excited," "worried or fearful," or "pleased or content." This practice of naming your emotions can help you make sense of them and communicate them more effectively to others.

3. **Understand Your Triggers**: Pay close attention to what triggers certain emotions for you. Is it a particular situation, person, or thought? When you understand your triggers, it can help you anticipate and prepare for any emotional reaction. It can also help you identify patterns in your emotions and behavior. For instance, maybe you are angry with your friend

not because he didn't show up for a game night but because he didn't trust you to share the reason for not coming to your place and informing you in advance. Knowing what triggered you can help you come up with a better response.

4. **Put Your Problem into Perspective**: Not every problem needs to be a big deal. Learn to tell the difference between major issues and minor annoyances. Not all problems are worth getting worked up over.

5. **Learn from Others**: There is a lot you can learn from people who have experienced the same problems you are facing. Talk to people who have been through tough times. It can be your parents, your elder sibling, or any trusted adult. Their experiences can teach you some really important stuff. Share your struggles with them and see what advice they have.

6. **Be Compassionate to Yourself**: Sometimes, we act too critical of ourselves, and we do not extend the compassion that we show to others. We need to give ourselves room to breathe and explore new experiences without judging our actions all the time. Accept the fact that it is normal to experience a range of emotions. In difficult situations, put yourself in your friend's position and imagine what advice you would give to them and how you would console them, then use similar words to talk to yourself with compassion.

7. **Be Patient:** It is okay to have bad days. Not every day has to be awesome and super productive. You can always bounce back from tough times, and that surely takes time. It is normal to have ups and downs. The important thing is to keep moving forward, even if it is one step at a time.

8. **Cultivate Gratitude**: Even when things are tough, there is always something to be grateful for. Take a moment to think

about the good things in your life, no matter how small. What helps me the most is that every night, when I get into bed, I list all the things I am grateful for in my mind. This practice instantly puts me in a better mood, and the next day, I get up feeling more motivated and energized. You can do the same.

9. **Choose Contentment over Happiness:** It is said that happiness is a temporary feeling that might come and go, but peace or contentment of heart is a deeper emotion that stays for a longer time. When you choose peace over pleasure, you find a deeper sense of satisfaction. Choose to be content with what you have and focus on the positives, even in challenging situations. You might not be able to control what happens to you, but you can control how you react.

10. **Seek Therapy When Needed:** It is totally cool to reach out for help if you are feeling stressed, anxious, down, or just not yourself. Seriously, no shame in the game! Whether it is talking to your school counselor, seeing a therapist, or consulting a medical expert, it is all good. These professionals are like the superheroes of coping strategies. They have tons of smart tricks up their sleeves to help you deal with whatever is going on. Plus, they are there to teach you those awesome techniques so you can tackle tough times like a boss. So, don't sweat it if you are struggling. Consult your counselors and therapists, they have your back!

Cognitive Structuring for Emotional Resilience

In simple words, cognitive restructuring is the process of organizing and reframing your thoughts. Think of it like organizing your phone's apps into folders. When you first get your phone, all the apps are scattered everywhere, right? It is chaotic and hard to find what you need. But when you start organizing them into folders, one for games, one for social media, and one for school stuff, it becomes much easier to find what you are looking for.

Similarly, in cognitive structuring, you organize your thoughts and ideas into imaginary "folders" in your brain. When you are faced with a problem or a stressful situation, your thoughts might be all over the place, and that makes it hard to focus and come up with a solution. But if you take a moment to organize your thoughts, break the problem into smaller bits, find connections between ideas, and ask yourself questions, then it will help you put your thoughts into neat little folders. Suddenly, everything starts feeling more manageable, and you can approach the situation with a clearer mind and a better plan of action.

When we face challenges or stressful situations, our thoughts can sometimes get jumbled up and overwhelmed. In such circumstances, our cognitive restructuring capabilities help us assess the causes, problems, and their possible solutions by organizing our thoughts. This way, we can quickly find the most suitable action plan to bounce back and fight the challenges without getting overwhelmed. This whole process pushes the stress and tension out of the picture, which significantly improves our emotional well-being and makes us more resilient. Now, let's understand how you can practice cognitive restructuring through a step-by-step process:

1. First, identify the negative thoughts. If you are feeling too stressed and anxious, then ask yourself why that is so. Let's say you are feeling stressed, worried, or anxious, and you are thinking: "I'm going to fail this presentation, and everyone will think I am a total failure." Your negative thought, in this case, is the fear of failure.

2. The next step is to counter and challenge this thought by asking yourself, "Is there any evidence to support this thought?" And if you assess the actual facts, you will realize that you have

prepared well for the presentation and you have also nailed it in the past. So, the reason behind your stress is not the lack of preparation but the fear of judgment, self-doubt, or perfectionism.

3. Now that you know the cause of negative thinking, you can fight it by thinking of an alternative positive thought. Like in the given scenario, you can tell yourself, "I have put in a lot of effort to prepare for this presentation, and I have succeeded in similar situations before. Even if I make a mistake, it doesn't mean I am a failure."

4. If you don't believe your counter thoughts, then evaluate this positive spin by thinking about your past experiences. Think about it! If you hadn't been that good in your past academic endeavors, getting into high school would not have been possible. You are concerned about your presentation, and that is a testament of your commitment to your studies.

5. Similarly, in different scenarios, continue practicing such positive self-talk to convince yourself of your capabilities. Be your own advocate for talking yourself out of negative thinking.

6. The process of structuring and restructuring your thoughts is ongoing; keep evolving your mindset and act according to each situation to reframe your thoughts. You will become the master of your mind and captain of your life.

Creative Ways to Release Emotional Tension

We often face triggers that can mess with our heads and tense our emotions. It is totally natural and happens to everyone, much like those storm clouds that roll in every now and then, but guess what? You have the power to make them disappear. Instead of letting that tension build-up, why not release it through creative outlets?

Using Creative Ways: Have you ever tried doodling when you are feeling down? Or writing a song or poem about how you are feeling? Even jamming with your favorite tunes and dancing around your room can put you in a great mood! Your emotions need a colorful outlet to get out of your system. Let's say you had a rough day at school. Instead of stewing in those feelings, you can just grab your sketchbook and start doodling. Before you know it, you will turn those negative vibes into a cool piece of art!

In a social media post, Zendaya, the famous star from Euphoria, revealed coloring as her favorite stress-releasing activity. According to her, she had a coloring station in her home, and she said: **"In my house, we all find it quite therapeutic. It helps me with stress."**

Talk It Out: You know that friend who is always there to listen? Well, don't be afraid to spill the beans and share what's on your mind. Talking about your feelings is another creative way to lift a weight off your shoulders and make things feel a whole lot lighter. If you are feeling super stressed about an upcoming test, talk with your bestie about it. Just talking it through helps you realize you are not alone, and suddenly, things don't seem so scary anymore.

Laugh It Off: They say laughter is the best medicine, and it is true! Watching a funny movie, sharing jokes with friends, or even just letting out a good belly laugh can instantly boost your mood and melt away stress. If you are feeling super tense after a long day of studying, then gather your friends for a movie night on a weekend. As you will all laugh together at the silly jokes on screen, you will feel the stress melting away.

Take a Break: Sometimes, all you need is a moment to pause, breathe and be present. Find a sense of peace amidst the ongoing chaos. Whenever you feel overwhelmed by all the stuff on your to-do list, your school projects, upcoming presentations, or exams, set aside a weekend to relax and unwind. Going out and connecting with nature really helps.

With every breath, you will feel more focused and totally ready to handle whatever challenges life throws your way.

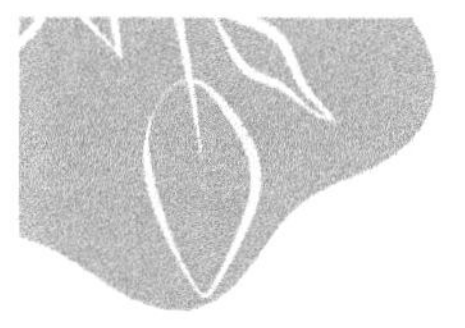

MINDFUL
NATURE
WALK

Let's take a chill walk in nature and really tune in to what is around us.

Materials Needed:

- Comfy shoes
- Weather-appropriate clothes
- Water bottle (it is good to stay hydrated)

How To Do It?

- Pick a day when the weather is nice and plan for a laid-back walk in a park, in the woods, or by the beach.

- Before you start, think about what you want to get out of this walk. Maybe it is just to relax and enjoy nature, or perhaps you want to clear your mind or notice things you usually overlook.

- Let's gather up your thoughts and take a few deep breaths to get in the zone.

- Walk at a pace that feels good to you, and pay attention to each step and how it feels.

- As you walk, really soak up what is around you.

- Look around and notice the colors, shapes, and textures of everything. Take in the sunlight dappling through the leaves or any animals you spot.

- Listen out for the sounds of nature: birds singing, leaves rustling, or water flowing. Try to hear even the quietest noises.

- Take deep breaths and smell the air. Observe any scents, such as the earthy smell after a rain or the sweetness of flowers.

- Reach out and touch things mindfully feel the roughness of tree bark, the softness of moss, or the coolness of a stream

- After returning home, you can write about this experience in a journal to reflect on how it made you feel and how you can make it even better the next time.

Are you ready to take that walk? With every step you take, you will feel tension leaving your body. It is not just the walk; all the other techniques that you have learned through the text of this chapter are lifesavers when it comes to dealing with stress. Start practicing them today, and you will experience a major change in your way of seeing the world, and your whole thought process will transform. You just have to believe in yourself, cultivate gratitude, and employ emotion regulation exercises to keep the reign of your life in your hands.

CHAPTER 9

Mastering Personal Hygiene and Self-Care Habits

"Your body is a temple, but only if you treat it as one."

— **Astrid Alauda**

A healthy mind and body are the greatest resources a person can have. You can learn, explore, and achieve all your life goals only when you are healthy. Our body requires constant care and support to stay active, healthy, and in shape. That is where self-care habits, taking care of personal hygiene, and eating and cooking healthy food come in.

Let's imagine your life learning any of those skills! What would happen? Right now, you may have the support of your parents or guardian, but soon, you will head to college or start living independently. Without these essential skills, your life will become chaotic, disorganized, and even messed up. Your health will be compromised by not caring for your hygiene and relying on unhealthy street or fast-food options.

Whereas, if you follow a personal hygiene routine, it will not only maintain your health but also boost your confidence and self-esteem.

When it comes to self-care, you need to put your mental and physical health at the top of your priority list. It makes you handle life's curveballs like a champ and become stronger, happier, and more resilient. So don't let your "I will deal with it later" mindset stop you from developing the most essential life skills you could ever learn. Trust me! These are going to be life-savers throughout your adulthood.

Why Is Personal Hygiene Important During Teenage?

Personal hygiene might seem basic, but it is super important. In the daily hustle of school life, it is easy to let it slip under the radar, but trust me, overlooking it can lead to all sorts of health problems. From pesky pimples to funky body odor, poor hygiene not only affects your physical health but also shatters your self-confidence. Perhaps personal hygiene is important because:

It prevents skin troubles: Your skin needs the most care when dealing with the changes that puberty throws your way during your early teenage years. Suddenly, your skin turns oily, and acne starts haunting you. It is high time to treat your skin with special care and wash your face and body regularly to keep pimples at bay and maintain healthy and glowing skin.

It keeps you healthy: As you get older, you will probably find yourself hanging out with friends more often and getting involved in all sorts of fun activities. But with more socializing comes a higher risk of picking up germs and getting sick. This is where good hygiene habits come in, like washing your hands regularly. Keeping clean can help lower your chances of catching illnesses and spreading them to others.

It makes you feel confident: Let's face it! When you are clean and fresh, you just feel better about yourself. Good hygiene can boost your confidence and make you feel more comfortable when you are around others. With this newfound confidence, you will probably find more people getting drawn towards you. People always love to hang out with someone who smells nice and looks presentable.

It deals with bodily changes: Your teenage years are a time of big changes, both physically and emotionally. From dealing with body hair to managing body odor, practicing good hygiene can help you feel more in control of these changes and less self-conscious about them.

It helps you stay focused: Believe it or not, taking the time to look after yourself can actually help you stay focused and on track with your goals. When you are clean and fresh, your confidence gets a boost.

Why Do Teens Face Personal Hygiene Issues?

Do you face any personal hygiene challenges? It is okay to admit it; we all struggle with it sometimes, especially when life gets super busy with all the academic, social, and extracurricular activities. Maybe you are finding it hard to stick to a consistent skincare routine, or perhaps you are forgetting to brush your teeth before bed. Whatever it is, remember that you are not alone. We are all in this together, and sometimes, just talking about our challenges can be the first step toward finding solutions. Let's address one issue at a time!

Hormonal Changes: Hormonal changes during adolescence can lead to increased oil production, which can cause skin issues like acne. Dealing with these teenage changes can be tough, and it might take some time to figure out how to keep our skin clear and healthy. If you are having acne issues, you should consult a skin specialist and get some skincare products prescribed according to your skin type to counter those skin problems.

Lack of Awareness: Sometimes, we just don't know any better! Personal hygiene is assumed to be so basic that in most households, it might not be considered something to be taught about or something to think about. But don't worry, knowledge is power, and learning about the importance of good hygiene habits can help us take better care of ourselves.

Procrastination: Let's face it, sometimes we would rather like to spend our time doing anything other than washing our face or brushing our teeth. Procrastination can be challenging, but establishing a routine and prioritizing personal hygiene can help us stay focused.

Delay in Cognitive Development: Our brains are still developing during our teenage years, and sometimes, it takes a while for us to grasp the importance of certain habits, like personal hygiene. As we grow and mature, we become more aware of the impact our actions have on our health and well-being.

Types of hygiene

Aristotle famously said, ***"Quality is not an act, it is a habit.*** " Once you develop a habit, no challenge will feel big enough to stop you from staying hygienic and well-groomed. You just need to be more consistent with your routine. In fact, there are plenty of super easy things you can gradually incorporate into your daily life to make a big difference.

Showering or Bathing: The simplest thing to do is take a shower or bath every day. It helps wash away dirt, sweat, and germs, keeping your skin clean and smelling good. Add bathing as a mandatory act to your morning or evening routine. You can set up a time for bathing according to your daily schedule. Skim through the following additional tips to amp up your shower game!

- Don't just stick to one soap or body wash. Experiment with different scents and formulas to find what works best for you. You might discover a new favorite!

- If you are sweating it out in sports or exercising, it's super important to rinse it off right after. It helps prevent body acne and keeps you feeling fresh.

- Once a week, grab a gentle exfoliating scrub to get rid of dead skin cells. It will leave your skin smoother and brighter.

- Don't skip the moisturizer after your shower, especially if you have dry skin. Choose one with hydrating ingredients such as shea butter or coconut oil.

- Those poufy loofahs might seem fun, but they can harbor bacteria. Opt for a washcloth or silicone body brush instead and wash them regularly.

- While you are in the shower, don't forget about your hair! Use shampoo and conditioner that suit your hair type, and consider a weekly hair mask for extra nourishment.

Washing Hands: Our hands touch all sorts of things throughout the day, so a simple act of washing them regularly with soap and water or using hand sanitizers goes a long way in preventing the spread of germs and keeps us from getting sick. Try these easy hacks to keep your hands germ-free.

- Don't just rush through washing your hands. Sing your favorite chorus or count to 20 while scrubbing to make sure you are getting rid of all those nasty germs.

- Washing your hands a lot can dry them out, especially if you are using hand sanitizer. Keep a travel-sized moisturizer handy to avoid lizard skin.

- Not all hand sanitizers are created equal. Look for ones with at least 60% alcohol to really zap those germs away.

- Keep a mini hand sanitizer attached to your backpack or purse for when you are out and about. You never know when you will need it!

- If you are using public restrooms, use a paper towel to turn off the faucet and open the door after washing your hands. It's like an extra layer of germ defense.

- Your hands might be clean, but your phone? Not so much. Give it a wipe-down with an alcohol-based screen cleaner every now and then to keep it germ-free.

Hair Care: When dirt, mixed with skin oil, is left on the scalp, it can cause dandruff or hair fall issues. The best way to avoid it is to wash your hair regularly with a superb quality shampoo with the least amount of harmful chemicals. Here are some other quick tips to keep your hair healthy:

- We all love a good hair straightener or blow dryer, but too much heat can dry out your scalp and lead to dandruff. Use heat styling tools on a lower setting, or give your hair a break every now and then.

- When you are shampooing, take some extra time to massage your scalp with your fingertips. It helps to stimulate blood flow and distribute natural oils, keeping your scalp healthy.

- On days when you are not washing your hair, dry shampoo is your best friend. It soaks up excess oil and gives a fresh boost to your hair without the need for water.

- If your hair roots are oily but your ends are dry, then apply conditioner only from mid-length to the ends of your hair. This way, you are moisturizing the driest parts without weighing down your roots.

- After shampooing and conditioning, finish by rinsing your hair with cold water. This helps seal the hair cuticle, adds shine, and feels refreshing!

- Certain vitamins, like biotin and vitamin E, can promote hair health. Consider adding a supplement to your routine or eating foods rich in these nutrients, like nuts, avocados, and eggs.

Dental Care: Want to have that great smile and avoid cavities, gum disease, and bad breath? Then, start taking your oral hygiene seriously. Brush your teeth after every meal, and regularly use floss. Brushing and flossing are your best friends in the fight against cavity drama and bad breath. But that's not all!. Follow these oral hygiene practices to maintain clean teeth and gums:

- Aim to brush for at least two minutes each time. Set a timer or play your favorite song to make sure you are giving your teeth a thorough clean.

- Scrubbing too hard can actually damage your gums and enamel. Use gentle, circular motions when brushing to avoid irritation.

- Don't forget to brush your tongue too! It's where a lot of bacteria hang out, causing bad breath. A quick scrub will keep your breath fresh.

- Flossing isn't just about getting food out from between your teeth. It also removes plaque buildup, which can lead to cavities and gum disease. Make it a daily habit!

- After brushing, rinse with mouthwash for an extra clean feeling. Look for one with fluoride to help strengthen your enamel and fight cavities.

- If you are unable to brush after a meal, consider chewing sugar-free gum to stimulate saliva production. This natural process cleanses your mouth and neutralizes acids, keeping your breath feeling fresh.

Shaving: If you are a guy who just started shaving, make sure to do it regularly to keep your skin smooth and stubble-free. Buy and use some quality shaving gel or cream to protect your facial skin from any potential irritation. Moreover, follow these simple techniques:

- Before you shave, splash your face with warm water, or shave after a hot shower. It helps open up your pores and soften your hair, making it easier to shave.

- Use a gentle face scrub a couple of times a week to remove dead skin cells. It helps prevent ingrown hair and gives you a smoother shave.

- When shaving, always go in the direction your hair grows. Shaving against the grain can cause irritation and razor bumps.

- Use short, light strokes instead of long, heavy ones. It gives you more control and reduces the risk of cuts.

- Keep your razor clean by rinsing it after every swipe. It prevents buildup and gives you a closer shave.

- After shaving, splash your face with cold water to close your pores. Then, apply a soothing aftershave or moisturizer to keep your skin hydrated and irritation-free.

- Don't wait too long to change your razor blade. A dull blade can cause nicks and irritation. Swap it out regularly for a clean, smooth shave.

Skincare: Your skin needs care. Facial skin is quite sensitive, and it must be taken seriously. Use a good facewash that suits your skin type (oil, dry, or in between); also, make sure to use skincare products that have "hyaluronic acid" in them to keep your skin moisturized. Go the extra mile and follow these tips to keep your skin glowing:

- Drinking lots of water is key. It helps keep your skin hydrated from the inside out, making it look clear and healthy.

- Sunscreen isn't just for summer. Apply it every day to protect your skin from harmful UV rays, which can cause damage and aging.

- Look for products with hydrating ingredients like hyaluronic acid, and avoid anything with mercury, parabens, or harsh sulfates.

- Don't overload your face with too many products. Stick to a simple skincare routine: cleanse, moisturize, and protect. Too many products can irritate your skin.

- Before you start using a new product, do a patch test on a small area of your skin. It helps you see if you will have a bad reaction without affecting your whole face.

- Change your pillowcase regularly. It collects oils and bacteria from your skin and hair, which can cause breakouts.

- Avoid touching your face too often throughout the day. Your hands carry dirt and germs that can cause pimples and other skin issues.

It is also important to avoid any product that may contain harmful chemicals like mercury. Make sure to consult a dermatologist before buying and applying any skincare product.

Nail Care: Germs love to hang up under your nails, so make sure you are giving them a good scrub too. Use a nail brush or even just your other hand's fingernails to clean them out. Keep those nails trimmed so that both the dirt and bacteria won't build up underneath them. And if you are a girl who likes to paint her nails, make sure to remove old polish before putting on a fresh coat on top to avoid any funky smells or infections.

- Keep your nails short and neat. Long nails are cool, but they can trap more dirt and bacteria, leading to infections.

- To keep your nails and cuticles moisturized, use cuticle oil or even a bit of coconut oil. It helps prevent them from getting dry and cracked.

- If you use nail clippers or files, make sure to clean them regularly. Germs can stick to these tools and spread to your nails.

- Look for breathable nail polish formulas. They allow more oxygen to reach your nails, keeping them healthier.

Toilet Hygiene: Again, it is super basic, and most of us are familiar with proper toilet hygiene, but we often overlook the importance of using a good anti-bacterial hand wash after using the bathroom. Here is how you can take care of your hygiene in both private and public bathrooms.

- Always use an anti-bacterial hand wash after using the bathroom. It is a game-changer for keeping your hands germ-free.

- If the bathroom doesn't have seat covers, layer some toilet paper on the seat before sitting down. It is an easy way to avoid germ contact.

- If available, use a tissue or paper towel to touch the flush handle in public restrooms to avoid direct contact with your hands.

- Push doors open with your elbow instead of your hands to avoid touching dirty door handles.

- Keep a mini hand sanitizer clipped to your bag or keychain. Use it right after washing your hands, especially in public bathrooms, for extra protection.

- Make sure that you dry your hands completely with a paper towel or hand dryer. Damp hands spread germs more easily.

Note: Skip ahead to the next part if this topic doesn't apply to you.

Menstrual Hygiene: Maintaining good hygiene practices during your period is crucial for comfort and health. Here are some essential tips:

- **Change Products Regularly**: Use period products (pads, tampons, liners, cups, or period underwear), depending on your flow, and change them frequently. (Word of caution: change the pads and liners every 3-4 hours and tampons and cups every 4-8 hours. Using any product longer than the recommended duration may cause skin irritation or infections)

- **Proper Disposal:** Dispose of used products hygienically in designated bins. Never flush them down the toilet.

- **Cleanse Gently:** Wash the **vulva** (the external genital area) with clean and lukewarm water throughout the day to avoid any infection. Avoid harsh soaps, which can disrupt the natural balance.

- **Hand Hygiene:** Wash your hands thoroughly before and after handling menstrual products to avoid the spread of bacteria.

- **Comfort Measures:** Taking long, warm baths during this time can help relieve cramps and promote relaxation, and it would be good for your hygiene as well.

Laundry Hygiene

Finding something nice and clean to wear out of that heap of clothes resting on a chair or in the corner of your room is really a daunting task. We have all been through this! It seems impossible to find a good pair of jeans or a shirt to wear to school, so you end up wearing the same old clothes over and over again. Do you want to avoid dealing with this mess? Then, create a system to wash, dry, fold, and iron your clothes in a timely manner so that every time you open your wardrobe, you will instantly find the perfect apparel to wear for the day. You can do your laundry over the weekends to keep the clothes ready for the coming week. Trust me! This practice will save a lot of your time during the week when you will have other important tasks to take care of. Here is how you can manage your dirty laundry:

Make Piles: First, separate your laundry into different piles based on color (lights, darks, whites) and fabric type (delicates, towels, jeans) and wash them separately, in batches, to prevent colors from bleeding and fabrics from getting damaged.

Remove Those Stains Right Away: Treat tough stains as soon as you can. The older a stain gets, the more difficult it gets to remove it. You can use a good stain remover or pre-treatment product to remove the stain before putting the clothes in the washer. Follow the instructions on the stain remover and test it on a small area of the fabric first to make sure it doesn't cause damage.

Load the Washer: Every washer has a certain capacity, and you need to add as many clothes as suggested in the instruction manual of the machine. If you overload the washer, it may not only cause damage to the machine but also to your clothes. Use the correct water temperature and cycle settings for the type of fabric and level of soiling.

Detergent and Softener: Read the instructions on the detergent packaging and use the amount suggested there. Add any of your favorite fabric softeners or some dryer sheets to the washer to give a fresh scent to clothes and keep them free from static.

Wash the clothes: Start the washing machine and let it complete the full cycle before removing the clothes. Use cold water for dark and bright-colored clothes so that their color won't fade away. Use warm water for whites and heavily soiled items.

Dry them Up: Shake out clothes before putting them in the dryer to prevent wrinkles. Check garment labels for drying instructions and use the appropriate heat setting. Remove clothes as soon as the dryer completes its cycle to prevent wrinkles and minimize static cling.

Fold and Iron: Fold clothes neatly as soon as they come out of the dryer to prevent wrinkles. Iron clothes as needed to remove wrinkles and creases. While ironing your clothes, keep the following few precautions in mind:

1. Switch on the iron with a lower heat setting and then gradually increase it as needed, especially for delicate fabrics such as chiffon, organza, silk, or wool.

2. Iron clothes inside out whenever possible to prevent shiny marks or damage to delicate fabrics.

3. Work in small sections and press the iron firmly but not too hard to avoid stretching the fabric.

4. Use the steam function if your iron has it, but avoid using it on synthetic fabrics, as excessive moisture can leave water stains,

5. Keep a pressing cloth or clean cotton cloth between the iron and delicate fabrics to protect them from direct heat.

6. For stubborn wrinkles, try spraying the fabric lightly with water before ironing.

7. If you accidentally create shiny marks on any fabric, place a neat, damp cotton cloth over the area and press it with a warm iron to remove the shine.

8. Hang or fold clothes neatly after ironing to prevent any wrinkles.

9. Let the ironed clothes cool completely before wearing or storing them.

10. Unplug the iron when not in use and keep it away from your younger siblings.

Now that we have covered the importance of personal hygiene and how maintaining cleanliness can impact your overall well-being, let's expand our focus to self-care. While personal hygiene is a crucial aspect of looking after yourself physically, self-care encompasses a broader spectrum, including mental and emotional health. By integrating effective self-care practices into your routine, you can have a balanced and holistic approach to maintaining your overall well-being.

Self-Care and Its Importance

We often hear the words "Take good care of yourself," but how much exactly do we take care of ourselves? Every time we are given a choice to choose healthy over unhealthy, we choose the latter because it sounds tempting or irresistible. Compromising sleep over late-night social media scrolling, choosing fast food over a healthy bowl of salad, and not doing regular exercise just because we feel lazy are just a few ways we put our health at risk. Self-care practices help us make better decisions and let us improve our mental and physical health in the long run. Now, it might sound like a fancy term, but it is super important, especially during these years of adolescence. Here is why it matters:

It prevents anxiety and stress: As you get through school, social life, and everything else, it is easy to feel overwhelmed. Self-care practices like deep breathing, mindfulness, or even just taking a break to do something you enjoy can help release anxiety and stress.

It keeps depression at bay: You are not immune to feeling down sometimes. Taking care of yourself means that you recognize when you are not feeling great and when you should seek support. Whether it is talking to a trusted adult, a counselor, or even a friend, reaching out is a crucial part of self-care.

It counters low self-esteem: Puberty can be a difficult time for your self-confidence. Self-care helps you nurture a positive relationship with yourself. It helps you celebrate your strengths, stay kind to yourself when things don't go as planned, and surround yourself with people who lift you up.

It protects you from social media: It is no secret that social media can mess with your head. Remember, what you see online is not always reality. Self-care helps you set boundaries with social media, take breaks when it becomes overwhelming, and focus on real-life connections.

It keeps your relationships healthy: Whether it is with friends, family, or crushes, relationships can be both amazing and challenging. Self-care also lets you set boundaries in relationships, helps you communicate openly, and allows you to walk away from toxic situations.

Types of Self-Care Activities for You

Self-care is not selfish; it is super essential for your well-being. There are numerous self-care practices that can maintain your physical, mental, and emotional well-being. You must experiment with several self-care practices to see which ones suit you the best. Once you select different activities, you can then create a self-care regimen to improve your resilience and manage stress for your general well-being.

1. Physical Self-Care: The most obvious form of self-care is taking care of the body. This means to engage in various healthy practices, such as:

- Get active every day, whether it is playing sports, dancing, or going for a walk. Find something you enjoy that gets your body moving.

- Fuel your body with nutritious foods that provide you energy and keep you feeling good. Ensure that your diet is balanced with plenty of fruits, veggies, and whole grains.

- Drink plenty of water throughout the day to keep your body hydrated. It's essential for staying healthy and feeling your best.

- Make sure you are getting enough sleep each night. Your body needs time to rest and recharge, so aim for 7-9 hours of shut-eye.

- Don't forget to take breaks throughout the day, especially if you are sitting for long periods. Stretch, walk around, or do some quick exercises to keep your body happy.

- Pay attention to your posture when sitting and standing. Sitting up straight can help prevent back and neck pain.

- If you are feeling tired or sore, give yourself permission to rest. Pushing yourself too hard can result in burnout or injury.

2. Emotional Self-Care: Your emotions affect your daily activities. So, it is just as important to take care of your emotions as you take care of your body. For emotional self-care, you can try activities like:

- Take a few minutes every day to practice mindfulness. This can be as simple as focusing on your breathing or paying attention to the present moment.

- Write down your thoughts and feelings in a journal as it is a great way to express yourself and understand your emotions.

- Don't be afraid to talk to someone you trust about how you are feeling. Whether it is a friend, family member, or counselor, sharing your emotions can help lighten the load.

- Surround yourself with positivity. Spend time with people who lift you up and engage in activities that bring you joy.

- Get creative! Whether it's through art, music, or writing, expressing yourself creatively can be incredibly helpful.

- Learn to say no to things that drain your energy or make you feel overwhelmed. It's okay to prioritize your own well-being.

- Be kind to yourself. Treat yourself with the same compassion you would show to a friend who is struggling.

- Take time to check in with yourself regularly. Ask yourself how you are feeling and what you need in that moment.

3. Social Self-Care: The way we socialize with others greatly affects our health. By connecting with people, you can vibe with them and develop healthy and positive relationships with others.

- Don't forget about your family! Spend time with your parents, siblings, or other family members. Even if you are not always vibing, family time can be valuable.

- Don't be afraid to branch out and meet new people. Join clubs, teams, or groups where you can connect with others who share your interests.

- It is important to set boundaries with friends and family. Let them know what you are comfortable with and when you need space.

- Share your thoughts and feelings with someone you trust or family members. Opening up about your stress and anxiety can help you feel supported and understood.

- Be a positive force in your social circles. Offer support, encouragement, and kindness to those around you.

- Take a break from social media and screens. Spend time connecting with people face-to-face rather than through likes and comments.

- Give back to your community by volunteering. It's a great way to connect with others and make a positive impact.

4. Creative Self-Care: This form of self-care allows you to tap into the creative side of the brain and let the ideas flow to heal yourself. Such self-care includes activities like:

- Let your creativity flow by engaging in activities such as drawing, painting, or any form of art that ignites your passion. It is a great way to express yourself and relieve stress.

- Put on your favorite tunes, or even try making your own music. Music can be a powerful way to boost your mood and unwind.

- Grab a journal and jot down your thoughts and feelings, or even start writing a story or poem. Writing can be super therapeutic and help you make sense of your emotions.

- Dive into a good book or explore articles, blogs, or stories that interest you. Reading not only expands your mind but can also transport you to different worlds.

- Get crafty with DIY projects, or try your hand at making something new. Whether it's knitting, scrapbooking, or building, creating with your hands can be incredibly satisfying.

- Put on some music and dance like nobody's watching! Dancing is a fun way to let loose and release tension.

- Take your camera or phone and snap some photos of things that catch your eye. Photography allows you to see the world from a different perspective and capture moments to cherish.

- Get in the kitchen and experiment with cooking or baking. Trying out new recipes can be a delicious way to express yourself and treat yourself.

Building a Self-Care Routine

"Self-care is giving the world the best of you instead of what's left of you."

- Katie Reed

From your mind to your emotional health and physical well-being, every part of your existence requires care, and you can make that happen by consistently investing your time and energy in yourself. The best way to achieve good health is to set up a comprehensive self-care routine, and here is how you can do it:

Set your Priorities: Consider the different parts of your life that make the most impact - physical health, mental well-being, relationships, and hobbies. What do you want to focus on improving or maintaining? If you prioritize having fun and oversleeping, then your health will be affected negatively. Sure, playing games to unwind is important for every other teen, but ask yourself! Is it worth compromising your studies and your good night's sleep? No! Health always comes first. So, set a schedule to limit your playing time and balance it with other self-care practices.

Set practical and achievable health goals: Start by setting small, achievable goals for yourself. Think about what you want to accomplish in the short term and what you hope to achieve in the long run. If you have in mind that "I want to grow as a healthy and active adult who doesn't want to complain about her back pain and obesity when she turns 40," then you will feel motivated to work out even when you find it unnecessary at this age.

Make an actionable plan: Once you know what you want to focus on, create a weekly or daily schedule that includes time for self-care activities. This could be anything from exercising to spending time with friends to practicing mindfulness. You can even follow those 30-day self-care challenges to develop the habit of incorporating all the healthy activities in your life. By doing so, you can include meditation, mindfulness, physical exercises, bathing, listening to music/podcasts, reading books, or perhaps any activity that will make you feel good about yourself. Or you can create a daily self-care checklist to incorporate all the activities into your routine (like the one given below)

(Daily)
SELF-CARE

DATE ___ / ___ / ___

S M T W T F S

CHECKLIST

- ○ MAKE YOUR BED
- ○ TAKE YOUR MEDICATIONS & VITAMINS
- ○ SKINCARE ROUTINE
- ○ HEALTHY MEALS
- ○ GO FOR A WALK
- ○ CLEANING HOUSE
- ○ WASHING CLOTHES
- ○ LISTEN TO MUSIC
- ○ HAVE A POWER NAP
- ○ SOCIAL MEDIA BREAK

- ○ TAKE A LONG BATH
- ○ DO A FACE MASK
- ○ CALL A FRIEND OR FAMILY
- ○ MEDITATION
- ○ WATCH A MOVIE
- ○ CUDDLE A PET OR HUMAN
- ○ TRY A NEW RESTAURANT
- ○ MAKE TIME TO READ
- ○ TRY A NEW RECIPE
- ○ NO PHONE 30 MINS BEFORE BED

WORKOUT

- ○ CARDIO
- ○ WEIGHT
- ○ YOGA
- ○ STRETCH
- ○ REST DAY
- ○ OTHER

HOURS OF SLEEP (Hours)

1 2 3 4 5 6 7 8

WATER BALANCE (Glass)

1 2 3 4 5 6 7 8

THINGS THAT MAKE ME HAPPY TODAY

MOOD

ANGRY TIRED SAD GREAT FUN

Pay attention to what works: After trying out different activities, closely observe how each activity makes you feel. If something helps you feel calm and grounded, make a note of it and try to add that to your routine more often. Your self-care routine might need to change from time to time, but that is okay! Be willing to adjust your plan as needed and try out new things to see what works best for you.

Get support from loved ones: It is okay to get help from your family, friends, or a trusted adult and ask them for support and encouragement as you work on building your self-care routine. You can ask your parents to remind you to do your own laundry, go to bed early, or ask a friend to join you for a walk in the park. Their support really makes a difference.

Self-Care Practices When in School

Are you struggling to find time for self-care with your busy school routine? Don't fret! There are ways that can help you rejuvenate and unwind even during the school hours.

- **Stretch whenever you can**: Take a few minutes between classes to stretch your body. This can help relieve tension and keep you feeling energized throughout the day.

- **Listen to music**: Pop in your earbuds and listen to your favorite tunes during your class breaks for a few minutes. When you listen to soothing and relaxing music, it instantly relaxes your mind and boosts your mood.

- **Take a relaxing breath**: When you are feeling stressed or overwhelmed, take a moment to close your eyes and take a few deep breaths. As your breath enters and leaves your body, notice it flowing in and out. It helps you feel calmer.

- **Use mindful exercises**: Take a moment to observe your surroundings with curiosity and without judgment. Look around and notice all the different hues, shapes, and textures. This can help you feel more grounded and present.

- **Always stay hydrated**: Drink lots of water (around eight glasses or more) throughout the day to keep your body and brain super hydrated. When you don't drink enough water throughout the day, it can cause dehydration, and that makes you feel tired and irritable. So make sure to keep the water bottle handy and take sips regularly.

Overcoming Self-Care Challenges for Teens

The journey to practicing a self-care routine with consistency is filled with challenges. I never said it is going to be easy, but with clear goals in mind and a will to keep yourself healthy, you can really do it. You just need to power through the following challenges like a ninja.

Time Constraints: It is one big challenge to find time for yourself between school, extracurricular activities, and social life. It can feel like there is never enough time for self-care. Try prioritizing self-care activities just like you would with other responsibilities. Set aside specific time slots for self-care in your schedule, even if it is just a few minutes each day. If you are consistent in your efforts, then even a 30-minute self-care session is enough to keep you fit and active.

Peer Pressure: It is quite common to feel pressure from friends or classmates to act a certain way or participate in activities that might not align with your values. Remember that it is okay to say no to things that don't feel right to you. Surround yourself with friends who support and uplift you, and don't be afraid to stand up for yourself. If you know in your heart that drinking is not good for your health, then don't let peer pressure change your mind and avoid those gatherings that might tempt or force you into doing things that you really don't want to do.

Unrealistic Expectations: Whether it is the pressure to excel academically or to look a certain way, unrealistic expectations can take a great toll on your mental health. I would recommend you practice positive self-talk and constantly remind yourself that it is okay not to be perfect and that you are unique in your own ways. Set realistic goals that you can achieve practically and celebrate your wins along the way, no matter how small. You can try certain daily affirmations to boost your confidence and to cherish your individuality. Every day, stand in front of the mirror, look at yourself for a minute or a half, and say any of the following affirmations out loud:

Daily Dose of Positive Affirmations

You Can Use Every Day

01. I am one-of-a-kind, and that is my superpower.

02. I am loved and worthy.

03. I am worthy of love and acceptance just as I am.

04. I am valued and helpful.

05. I shine brightest when I embrace my true self.

06. I am safe and surrounded by love and support.

07. I am not meant to fit in; I am meant to stand out.

08. My uniqueness allows me to express myself authentically.

Feeling Guilty or Unworthy: It is easy to feel guilty or unworthy, especially when you are focusing on yourself instead of others. But here I would like to quote Eleanor Brown, who once said, ***"Self-care is not selfish. You cannot serve from an empty vessel,"*** and I couldn't agree more. You can only be there for others when you feel healthy, whole, and emotionally sound. So, be kind to yourself and practice self-compassion. You deserve to take care of yourself just as much as anyone else.

Challenges of Change: Change can be scary and overwhelming, whether it is transitioning to a new school, dealing with family changes, or navigating relationships. The fear of change or the evolving circumstances can often overwhelm you, which leaves you so distressed that you overlook your self-care regime. The best way to overcome this challenge is to lean on your support system for guidance and encouragement and remember that it is totally fine to ask for help when you need it.

There you have it! All the ways to master personal hygiene and self-care habits are packed in one chapter. By taking care of yourself inside and out, you are not just making sure you look and feel great, but you are also building important life skills that will stick with you forever. So, keep practicing those hygiene routines and taking time for self-care. You are on your way to becoming the ultimate boss of your own well-being!

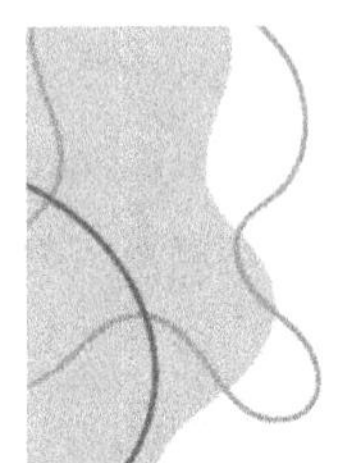

30 DAYS *Of*
SELF LOVE

Let's take this 30-days challenge and see the power of self-care transforming your life.

DAY 1	DAY 2	DAY 3	DAY 4	DAY 5
Start a gratitude journal	Learn to meditate	Spend the day social media free	Call someone you love	Take a 15 minute walk outdoors
DAY 6	**DAY 7**	**DAY 8**	**DAY 9**	**DAY 10**
Listen to a podcast	Learn to cook a new recipe	Stretch for 10-15 minutes	Listen to your favorite song	Practice deep breathing
DAY 11	**DAY 12**	**DAY 13**	**DAY 14**	**DAY 15**
Try a free online workout	Read a book for 15 minutes	Write a list of short-term goals	De-clutter a room or desk	Go to bed 30 minutes earlier
DAY 16	**DAY 17**	**DAY 18**	**DAY 19**	**DAY 20**
Have a game night	Wake up 15 minutes earlier	Make your favorite meal	Buy yourself something nice	Create a bucket list
DAY 21	**DAY 22**	**DAY 23**	**DAY 24**	**DAY 25**
Watch a movie or series	Write down your thoughts	Take a long shower or bath	Have a home spa day	Read inspirational quotes
DAY 26	**DAY 27**	**DAY 28**	**DAY 29**	**DAY 30**
Create a vision board	Spend some time outside	Do a hair mask	Spend time with loved ones	Take a power nap

CHAPTER 10

Health, Nutrition, and Kitchen Skills for Teens

"I think cooking is really key because it is the only way you are going to take back control of your diet."

– **Michael Pollan**

You are what you eat! Consuming organic and clean food keeps you healthy and disease-free. Let me ask you one thing: what would happen if you fill the tank of a high-performance sports car with low-quality fuel? It won't perform that well, right? Just like a car's engine requires optimum quality fuel to do its best, our body also needs the best quality food to do all kinds of activities.

With a good diet, you can say goodbye to all the chronic diseases and health issues. However, in this age of processed food, it is difficult to get perfectly cooked, healthy meals from outside. Sure, the things you buy from restaurants taste delicious at times, but not all places follow healthy cooking practices, and sometimes, you never know which ingredients they have used. So, the best way to avoid consuming those unhealthy dishes is to cook the healthy ones at home using fresh organic ingredients. Plus, eating out is a burden on your pocket as well. You can save a lot of money and protect your health by learning some basic kitchen skills, planning meals, and cooking at home.

These skills will come in handy when you join college, go camping, or start your adult life. Even in your teenage phase, you can put your cooking skills to use and surprise your loved ones with well-cooked homemade meals. It is one good way to stay healthy and save a lot of money from being spent on processed and unhealthy food.

Essential Skills to Get Started With

Now, the question is, what type of skills you must learn and practice before becoming a kitchen maestro? When you enter the kitchen, three things matter the most- food hygiene, safety, and culinary skills. This means that getting the food cooked is not the only goal here; you have to stay organized and careful with the tools to keep the food you cook and yourself safe from any disaster. Here are some basic skills that you should learn to practice from this age:

Slicing and Dicing

If you learn to slice and dice nicely, cooking will be a breeze. Get comfortable with a knife and practice how to chop veggies like a pro and dice like a chef. There are a variety of kitchen knives that you must be familiar with before you dice or slice an ingredient, such as:

- **Chef's Knife**: This one is a versatile knife for chopping, slicing, and mincing fruits, vegetables, and meats.

- **Paring Knife:** It is a small knife for intricate tasks like peeling, trimming, and slicing small fruits and vegetables.

- **Serrated Knife:** This one is ideal for slicing bread and delicate items like tomatoes without squishing them.

- **Utility Knife**: It is an all-purpose knife smaller than a chef's knife, perfect for various cutting tasks.

We all know that knives are sharp and dangerous; if you are not careful with them, they might leave you with a finger cut. Here are some easy ways to use your knives safely:

- Do not use dull or damaged knives.

- When you are holding a knife in your hand, make sure to keep your grip neither too tight nor too loose.

- Work on a stable cutting board placed on a flat surface.

- While cutting any vegetable, place it on a cutting board and hold it with one hand by curling your fingers under it and using knuckles to keep the knife edge away from the fingertips.

- Use a gentle sawing motion when cutting.

- Cut away from your body.

- Keep an eye on your surroundings and avoid any distractions at the time of cutting.

- Store knives safely in a designated holder.

- If you are new to cutting, then you can also try wearing a finger protector to practice your slicing and dicing skills.

Cooking Basics

Time to rock the stove! Practice your sautéing, stir-frying, boiling, baking, and grilling skills. Once you learn these skills, you can cook up almost anything. To cook a variety of dishes, you will have to use the following cookware:

- **Pots**: They are used for boiling, simmering, and cooking liquids such as soups, pasta, and sauces.

- **Pans/ frying pans/skillets**: Use them for frying, sautéing, and searing foods such as vegetables, meats, and eggs.

- **Baking Sheets:** They are basically flat trays that are used for baking cookies, roasting vegetables, and cooking meat in the oven.

- **Dutch Oven**: It is a type of deep pot with a lid made out of steel or iron, and it is often used for braising, stewing, and slow cooking,

Speaking of ovens, besides cookware, there are several cooking appliances that you may need to use in the kitchen on a regular basis, such as:

Oven: To use the oven, first preheat it to the specified temperature (according to the recipe) before placing food inside. If you want to keep your hands safe, always wear oven mitts to move hot pots and pans around the kitchen. Do not open the oven door frequently when the food is cooking inside, as this can cause temperature fluctuations and affect cooking times. Use a timer to keep track of cooking times and prevent overcooking. Clean the oven regularly to remove food residue and prevent smoke or odors.

Stove: To cook on the stove, use cookware with flat bottoms and lids that fit snugly to ensure even cooking and prevent spills. Adjust the burner to the desired heat level before placing the cookware on the stove. While cooking, use a pot holder or oven mitts to hold the hot pots and pans. Stir food occasionally to prevent sticking or burning. Turn off the burner when cooking is complete, and remove cookware from the stove.

Microwave: To heat food in the microwave, use microwave-safe containers and covers to prevent splatters. Place food evenly in the microwave and avoid overcrowding for thorough cooking. Use microwave-safe lids or vented plastic wraps to cover food and prevent steam buildup. Stir or rotate food halfway through cooking to promote even heating. Leave the cooked food at room temperature for a few minutes after cooking to allow for heat distribution and prevent burns.

Toaster: Place bread slices or other items in the toaster slots and select the desired toast setting. Use caution when removing toasted items, as they may be hot. Clean the toaster regularly to remove crumbs and prevent fire hazards. Avoid inserting metal objects into the toaster, as this can cause electrical hazards. Never leave the toaster unattended while in use.

Toaster Oven: Preheat the toaster oven to a specified temperature before placing food inside. Use oven-safe cookware and baking sheets when cooking in the toaster oven. Monitor food closely during cooking to prevent burning or overcooking. Do not touch the toaster directly when it's hot! Wear oven mitts in case you have to move the toaster around.

Washing and Preserving Fresh Produce

Fruits and veggies need special care as they can't stay fresh longer than 2-3 days. When you bring them home, you will have to wash and store them properly to prolong their storage life and preserve their flavors. Here are some effective ways to do that:

- Rinse fruits and vegetables with tap water once you bring them home.

- Use a produce brush for firm-skinned fruits and vegetables, like apples and potatoes.

- To clean those leafy greens, take a bowl of water and immerse them in it. Swish them gently to remove dirt. Lift and drain the greens in a colander, then rinse thoroughly with cold running water.

- After washing, spread the washed veggies and fruits on a clean cloth or paper towel to remove their excess moisture.

- Refrigerate all your fresh fruits and veggies to maintain their freshness, except for bananas, potatoes, onions, and garlic, which should be stored in a cool, dry place.

- Keep fruits and vegetables in separate containers to prevent them from ripening too quickly or absorbing odors from each other.

- Use airtight containers or produce bags to store cut fruits and vegetables in the refrigerator.

- Check stored veggies and fruits regularly to see any signs of spoilage, and discard any items that are moldy, mushy, or have a strong odor.

- Freeze fruits and vegetables for longer-term storage by washing, cutting, and placing them in freezer-safe bags or containers.

Know Your Ingredients

Get to know your ingredients! Learn how to prepare them, including washing, peeling, and chopping. Understand how each ingredient adds flavor to your dishes. Don't be afraid to experiment with different ingredients.

Recipe Reading

Let's crack open those cookbooks! Master the art of following recipes step by step. Cookbooks are a great way to learn and experiment with new and healthy recipes!

Meal Planning

Time to get organized! Plan out your meals, make shopping lists, and get everything ready before you start cooking. Some ways to plan your meals include:

- Set aside time each week to plan your meals and snacks. Go with recipes that are simple and easy to prepare.

- Jot down a list of all the items and ingredients you will need for the week based on your planned meals, and check what you already have in your pantry and refrigerator.

- Add a variety of foods from different food groups into your meals, including fruits, vegetables, whole grains, lean proteins, and healthy fats.

- Buy veggies and fruits that are available during the season, as they are cheaper and healthier than canned produce.

- Don't forget to include healthy snacks like fresh fruit, nuts, yogurt, or cut-up vegetables to keep you fueled between meals.

Get ready to think on your feet! Once you learn the basic skills, feel free to mix things up. Swap ingredients, try new flavors, and make the recipe your own.

Clean up after you cook

The party is not over until the kitchen is clean! Learn how to wash dishes and keep your cooking space sparkling clean. After all, kitchen hygiene is also important! Here are some tips to easily wash the dishes and to keep your kitchen clean:

- Scrap and throw out those leftover food bits before washing dishes so that your sink doesn't get blocked.

- If you have a two-sided sink, then fill one side with soapy water and the other with clean and warm water to rinse the dishes.

- Start by cleaning the dishes that are least dirty, like glasses and mugs, and then move to the dirtier ones, like pots and pans.

- Scrub dishes, utensils, and cookware with warm, soapy water using a sponge or dishcloth.

- Pay special attention to utensils and dishes with crevices or stuck-on food, using a scrub brush or sponge to clean thoroughly.

- Rinse dishes under warm, running water to remove soap residue.

- Place washed dishes on a dish rack or on a clean towel to air dry.

- Change dishwater if it becomes too dirty or soapy.

- Clean kitchen surfaces, including countertops and sinks, after washing dishes to maintain cleanliness.

Food Storage

If fresh food is left at room temperature, it gets spoiled within 12-24 hours, depending on the room temperature. This is why it has to be properly packed and stored in a refrigerator or freezer for prolonged freshness. Before storing the food, make sure to check if there are any signs of spoilage:

- If the food changes in color, texture, or odor, then it is no longer safe to eat it. It is best to throw it away.

- Discard any perishable foods that appear moldy, slimy, or have an off smell.

- Always check the expiration dates on packed foods and discard any product that has expired.

If your food is not spoiled and it is perfectly edible, you can safely store it in your refrigerator or freezer according to the following guidelines:

Refrigerator Storage

- The temperature inside the refrigerator must be 40°F (4°C) or below to slow down bacterial growth in perishable items.

- Always keep raw meat, poultry, and seafood on the bottom shelf of the refrigerator to keep their juices from dripping on top of other foods. This way, you avoid cross-contamination.

- Use or freeze fresh produce within a few days of purchase for the best flavors and nutritional value.

- Keep leftovers in airtight containers or resealable bags before storing them in the refrigerator. Consume leftovers within 3-4 days.

Freezing Guidelines

- Freeze food quickly to maintain quality and safety. Divide leftovers into smaller portions for quicker cooling before freezing.

- Label freezer bags or containers with the date and contents to keep track of what's in your freezer and when it was frozen.

- To prevent freezer burn and maintain the freshness of the food, store it in freezer-safe bags or containers.

- Follow these recommended freezing times for different types of foods:

    o Raw meat, poultry, and seafood: 2-6 months

    o Cooked meat, poultry, and seafood: 2-3 months

    o Soups, stews, and casseroles: 2-3 months

  o Bread and baked goods: 2-3 months

  o Fruits and vegetables: 8-12 months

Once the food is frozen, simply defrost it at room temperature and cook/reheat it on the stove or in the microwave to use and serve again.

Eating Balanced Meals

"Eat healthy"- we often hear and see those words everywhere, but seldom do we realize their importance and understand what they truly mean. A healthy diet is a balanced diet, free from processed and fast food. The purpose of a healthy diet is to provide you with all sorts of nutrients in the amount required by the body to grow healthily. During your teen years, your body goes through these massive changes, and you are constantly growing into a fine young adult, so it is high time to take care of your nutritional intake and keep track of the calories, carbs, proteins, fats, and other vitamins you consume. According to research, the total number of calories that boys and girls of your age must consume ranges from:

- Boys: 2,200 - 3,200 calories

- Girls: 1,800 - 2,400 calories

When food is metabolized, the energy released is measured in calories. The caloric requirements of the body depend on the build and size of the body, along with the intensity of the physical activity or exercises you engage in. These calories are sourced from a variety of nutrients present in the food we consume. The right mix of nutrients in every meal makes a diet more balanced and healthier. Here are the three major macro-nutrients that you must consume:

Carbohydrates

Our body needs glucose to function, and carbohydrates are the major source of glucose. This is why our body requires a good amount of carbs. Our diet must receive **45% to 65%** of carbs out of the total daily calories. There are several sources of carbs you can add to your diet, such as:

- **Fruit and Vegetables:** Try to add a variety of fresh and colorful fruits and veggies to your diet every day. These ingredients are packed with essential nutrients, vitamins, and antioxidants that support your growth and development. Add at least five servings of fruits and veggies to your meals and snacks each day, which can give you a good mix of nutrients.

- **Starchy Foods**: Instead of consuming fine flour, choose whole grains like oats, quinoa, brown rice, and whole wheat bread as your primary sources of carbohydrates. These foods are loaded with fiber, which is important for maintaining a healthy gut system and keeping you feeling full and satisfied.

Now, carbs can be good or bad, depending on the type of carbs you consume. Those sugary cola drinks, candies, fried food, fast food, white sugar, and market-packed baked goods contain refined carbs, which instantly spike our blood sugar level and cause various health problems in the long run, such as diabetes, obesity, hormonal imbalances, etc. Instead of such food items, you need to consume whole food, fresh fruits, vegetables, brown sugar, and other sources of complex carbs to keep your body nourished, healthy, and disease-free.

Proteins

Proteins contain amino acids that build our muscles and keep our hair, nails, and skin healthy. Proteins are different from carbs, and they have to be consumed in slightly different quantities to keep the body nourished. A balanced diet must contain **10-35% of the protein**s. They are important for building your muscles and keeping your nails and hair healthy. You can try a variety of sources to increase your daily protein intake:

- Beans

- Pulses

- Fish

- Eggs

- Lean meats

- Poultry

Protein is also essential for repairing tissues in your body, so make sure you are getting an adequate amount each day to support your growth and muscle development.

Fats

Fats are another important nutrient that contains more energy than carbs, and they help develop brain cells and run other body functions. A balanced diet must contain 20–35% of fat out of the total percentage. When it comes to fat sources, there are several natural ingredients that you can go for:

Dairy and Alternatives: Don't forget to add dairy products to your diet to make sure you are getting enough calcium for strong and healthy bones, whether it's milk, yogurt, or cheese. If you are lactose intolerant or vegetarian, then try alternatives like fortified plant-based milk like almond or coconut milk and yogurt (coconut or soy).

Oils and Spreads: While fats should be consumed in moderation, it is super important to use fats that are healthy. Olive oil, nuts, seeds, and avocados are some really good sources of healthy fats. These fats carry essential fatty acids that support brain function and overall health.

Micronutrients

Besides the above-mentioned major ingredients, our body also requires several other nutrients in a small amount, such as vitamins, minerals, and fiber. Even though they are required in a small amount, they are really important for our growth.

The following table gives you the optimum amount of both macro and micronutrients that you need on average, along with their respective sources:

Nutrient	Amount Required for a Balanced Diet	Common Sources
Calories	Boys: 2,200 - 3,200 calories Girls: 1,800 - 2,400 calories	Carbohydrates, proteins, fats
Carbohydrates	45-65% of total daily calories	Whole grains, fruits, vegetables, legumes
Proteins	10-30% of total daily calories	Lean meat, poultry, fish, eggs, legumes
Fats	25-35% of total daily calories	Avocado, nuts, seeds, olive oil, fatty fish
Calcium	1,300 mg per day	Dairy products, leafy greens, fortified foods
Iron	11-15 mg per day	Red meat, poultry, fish, fortified cereals
Vitamin D	600 IU per day	Sunlight, fatty fish, fortified foods
Vitamin A	700-900 mcg per day	Liver, sweet potatoes, carrots, spinach
Vitamin C	65-75 mg per day	Citrus fruits, strawberries, bell peppers
Vitamin B12	2.4 mcg per day	Meat, fish, dairy products, fortified foods
Folate	400 mcg per day	Leafy greens, legumes, fortified cereals
Fiber	25-38 grams per day	Whole grains, fruits, vegetables, legumes
Water	8-10 cups (64-80 ounces) per day	Water, fruits, vegetables, soups, teas

Navigate Grocery shopping

Grocery shopping is something that every person has to do at some point in life. The earlier you learn to shop like a pro, the easier your life will be. Smart grocery shopping can actually save a lot of money and time. So, why not start learning that now?

Make a List: Before you head to the store, take a paper and pen to jot down all the items you need. You can even create a list on your mobile, tablet, or laptop. With this list in your hand, you can avoid unnecessary purchases. Plus, it makes sure you don't forget anything important!

Create a Foolproof Meal Plan: Plan out all your meals for the week ahead of time. This way, you will know exactly which ingredients you need to buy, and you can avoid aimless wandering in the aisles.

Build a Colorful Cart: The more colors there are, the better it is! That's what they say about a plate and a grocery cart. So, fill your cart with a rainbow of fruits and vegetables. Choose a variety of colors to make sure that you are getting a wide range of nutrients. Plus, colorful produce is always fresher and more flavorful! Here are some tips to pick the right veggies and fruits for your cart:

- **Appearance:** Good quality fruits and veggies are firm, vivid in color, and free from bruises or blemishes, so choose them. Avoid vegetables and fruits that appear wilted, overripe, or have signs of spoilage.

- **Seasonality:** Go for seasonal fruits and vegetables whenever possible, as they tend to be fresher, more flavorful, and may be more affordable.

- **Texture:** Besides appearance, the texture of the fruits and vegetables also tells a lot about their quality. For example, leafy greens should be crisp and fresh, while root vegetables should feel firm and free from soft spots.

- **Smell:** Some vegetables, such as onions and garlic, should have a mild, fresh aroma. Avoid vegetables and fruits with strong or unpleasant odors, as it may be a sign of spoilage.

- **Storage:** Keep in mind how you plan to store and use the vegetables and fruits. Choose vegetables and fruits that will stay fresh for the duration you need them and can be stored properly in your refrigerator or pantry.

- **Weight:** Heavier fruits are often juicier and riper. Lift and compare similar fruits to choose the ones with the most weight for their size.

Read Food Labels: Take a moment to read the labels on the products you are considering buying. Pay attention to things like serving size, calories, carbs, preservatives, ingredients, and nutritional information. Some simple standards to check those values include:

- **Serving Size**: The serving size indicates the amount of food used to calculate the nutrient information on the label.

- **Total Calories:** This represents the total number of calories in one serving of the food. It gives you an idea of the energy content of the food.

- **Fats**: Saturated and trans fats contain bad cholesterol, so their consumption must be limited, while unsaturated fats are healthier choices.

- **Carbohydrates and Fiber**s: Choose foods high in fiber and opt for complex carbohydrates over simple sugars.

- **Protein:** Aim for foods with a moderate to high protein content to support the growth of muscles and overall health.

- **Added Sugar**: Added sugars contribute extra calories without providing any nutritional benefits. Donor adds food items that have added sugar to your cart.

- **Sodium:** High sodium intake is linked with high blood pressure and other health problems, so it is important to choose lower sodium options if possible.

Never Shop Hungry: One of the golden rules of grocery shopping is to never do it on an empty stomach. Never hit the grocery store empty stomach, or else you will end up buying things that are not on the list. So, before going to the grocery store, always eat something.

Set Your Spending Limit: Before you walk through those automatic doors, decide how much you are willing to spend. Having a budget in mind will help you prioritize your purchases and avoid overspending.

Quick and Easy Recipes

Entering into the kitchen knowing exactly which ingredients to use and how can be really helpful. It is best to start practicing your skills with some basic recipes and then refine your cooking skills over time. After practice, you can try more variations and add ingredients of your choice to explore your love for cooking. Here are some easy-peasy ideas to get you started with:

Berry Yogurt Smoothie- A Healthy Morning Delight

Preparation time: 5 minutes
Cooking time: 0 minutes
Serves: 1

Ingredients:

- 1 cup mixed berries (you can choose your favorite berries)
- 1/2 cup yogurt (it can be either plain or flavored)
- 1/2 cup milk
- 1 tablespoon honey/ maple syrup
- Ice cubes

Instructions:

1. Wash all your berries by rinsing them under tap water and remove their stems or leaves.
2. Add mixed berries, yogurt, milk, ice cubes, and honey or maple syrup to your blender jug and blend well until it is smooth.
3. Pour the smoothies into a glass and serve fresh.

Variation Tips:

- Want to add some more fiber to the smoothie? Add some spinach or kale to sneak in some extra greens. You won't even taste them!
- Boost the protein percentage of this smoothie by adding a spoonful of protein powder or some nut butter.
- For a creamier texture, substitute some or all of the milk with coconut milk or almond milk.
- Replace some of the berries with tropical fruits like mango, pineapple, or banana for a taste of the tropics.

Grilled Cheese Sandwich - Quick Lunch Meal

Preparation time: 5 minutes

Cooking time: 6 minutes

Serves: 1

Ingredients:

- o   2 slices of bread
- o   Butter
- o   2 slices of cheddar cheese

Instructions:

1. Put any suitable non-stick pan on the stove and turn its heat to medium.
2. Spread some butter over the top of a bread slice.
3. Put the buttered side of the bread slice down on the pan.
4. Placc a slice of cheese on top of this bread.
5. On top of the other bread slice, spread butter, then place it on top of the cheese with the buttered side facing up.
6. Let the sandwich cook for 2-3 minutes per side until golden brown.
7. Let it cool for a minute or two, then slice it in half if you like, and enjoy your delicious Grilled Cheese Sandwich!

Variation Tips:

- Add some protein by including sliced deli meats such as ham, turkey, or cooked bacon between the cheese slices.
- There are other cheeses like cheddar, mozzarella, Swiss, or pepper jack that you can try for unique flavor combinations.
- Boost the nutritional value by adding thinly sliced vegetables like tomatoes, bell peppers, onions, or spinach to the sandwich before grilling.

No Bake Energy Bites

Preparation time: 5 minutes
Refrigeration time: 30 minutes
Serves: 2

Ingredients:

- o   1 cup rolled oats
- o   1/2 cup peanut butter
- o   1/3 cup honey or maple syrup
- o   1/4 cup mini chocolate chips
- o   1/4 cup shredded coconut
- o   1 teaspoon vanilla extract
- o   Pinch of salt

Instructions:

1. Put all the ingredients in a bowl.
2. Mix everything together until it is all combined.
3. If it is too dry, add a bit more honey or peanut butter.
4. Use your hands to roll the mixture into small balls.
5. Put the balls on a plate or tray.
6. Put the plate or tray in the fridge for at least 30 minutes.
7. Once they are firm, they are ready to eat!
8. You can keep any extras in the fridge for up to a week.

Variations Tips:

- You can try adding different ingredients to change up the flavor of your energy bites! Here are some ideas:
- Add chopped nuts like almonds, walnuts, or pecans to the mixture for extra crunch and protein.
- Chopped raisins, cranberries, or dates can also be added to the mixture to create sweet and chewy bites.
- Stir in seeds such as chia seeds, flaxseeds, or sunflower seeds for added nutrition and a crunchy texture.

Microwave Mug Brownie - An Easy 2 minutes Dessert

Preparation time: 5 minutes
Cooking time: 2 minutes
Serves: 1

Ingredients:

- 4 tablespoons all-purpose flour
- 4 tablespoons sugar
- 2 tablespoons cocoa powder
- 3 tablespoons vegetable oil or melted butter
- 3 tablespoons water
- 1 egg
- Optional: chocolate chips or chopped nuts

Instructions:

1. In a microwave-safe mug, mix together the flour, sugar, and cocoa powder until well combined.
2. Add the vegetable oil or melted butter and water to the mug. Add egg to this mixture and stir until it turns smooth.
3. If desired, stir in some chocolate chips or chopped nuts for extra flavor and texture.
4. Place the mug in the microwave and cook on high for 1-2 minutes. The brownie will rise and set when it is done, but be careful not to overcook it.
5. Let the brownie cool for a minute before eating.
6. Serve and enjoy.

Now that you have a few basic recipes and an understanding of basic kitchen skills, it's about time to start practicing. Whether you start by making a glass of smoothie every morning or try to make a delicious cheese sandwich for you and your family, every dish you make will help you improve and polish your kitchen skills. Once you get the hang of it, you won't ever have to rely on market-bought unhealthy food products. If cooking really tempts you, then you can always buy online cookbooks or search for recipes on different websites to play with various ingredients. The idea is to become self-sufficient and reliant to live a healthy and fulfilling life ahead.

Activity

This week, try making a grocery list for your home and write down all the things required in the following organized manner. You can discuss the details with your parents and let them help you to understand the pantry requirements. After putting everything down on the list, go along with your parents to the grocery store and pick things up according to the grocery shopping tips shared in the previous chapter. Share your experience with your friends and family as well.

GROCERY SHOPPING LIST

MEAT / FISH / DAIRY	QTY

FRUITS & VEGETABLES	QTY

PANTRY ITEMS	QTY

FREEZER ITEMS	QTY

BEVRAGE & SNACKS	QTY

MISCELLANEOS	QTY

BONUS CHAPTER

Empowering Yourself - Raise as a Leader

"You have within you right now everything you need to deal with whatever the world can throw at you."

— **Brian Tracy**

Wyatt was a teenager with incredible skills in debating, problem-solving, and critical thinking. But he has always been held back by his own self-doubt. He never felt confident enough to show off his talents in school debate competitions or take charge of class projects. One day, Wyatt was hanging out with his uncle, who was a communication maestro. Wyatt opened up about how he struggled with self-doubt and how his uncle had dropped some serious wisdom on him. He told Wyatt that believing in himself was the key to unlocking his full potential. Inspired by his uncle's advice, Wyatt decided to take a leap of faith. He decided to join the debate club at school. At first, he was super nervous, I mean, who wouldn't be? But something amazing happened as he started debating and talking with his classmates.

Wyatt started feeling more confident. With each debate, he got better at expressing his ideas and thinking on his feet. His brain started firing on all cylinders, and he was able to tackle problems like a boss. And guess what? As Wyatt's confidence grew, he started stepping up in other ways too. He volunteered to lead group projects, came up with amazing solutions to tough problems, and inspired his classmates to do their best.

Before he knew it, Wyatt became a leader and a role model among his peers. His journey from self-doubt to self-belief taught him a major lesson: that with a little belief in yourself and a whole lot of determination, you can achieve anything. From that day on, Wyatt grabbed every chance he could get to show off his talents and lead with confidence. He didn't let self-doubt hold him back anymore. Instead, he learned to empower himself to reach for the stars.

So, Wyatt's story takes us back to what Brian Tracy has said! You really have all the potential within you. It just requires a little self-exploration and self-belief to acknowledge your capabilities, cherish and express them openly to let the world see you shine. And when you finally do that, empowerment follows you everywhere, and you become a leader for those who take inspiration from you.

Qualities of a Good Leader

Being a leader doesn't mean that you need to boss people around all day. It doesn't even come from a position of power. The ability to lead comes from a will to bring positive and constructive changes while leading the people around you in the right direction. You become a leader not to enjoy all its perks but to take on the responsibility of solving critical problems and helping others. So, besides self-belief, what makes a person a good leader? Here are some characteristics that are common among all leaders:

- **Good Communication Skills:** All good leaders know how to communicate effectively. They listen carefully to others, express their ideas clearly, and provide feedback in a constructive way.

- **Confidence**: It is a must! If you want to lead others, you definitely need to have confidence in yourself and your abilities. When you believe in yourself, others are more likely to trust and follow your lead.

- **Empathy**: Understanding and empathizing with others is another basic characteristic of effective leadership. A good leader is able to put oneself in other people's shoes, listen to their concerns, and offer support when needed.

- **Integrity:** Honesty and integrity are two crucial qualities for leaders. When you are honest and transparent, it builds trust between you and others and helps establish your credibility as a leader.

- **Vision**: Great leaders have a clear vision of where they want to go and how to get there. They inspire others with their vision and motivate them to achieve common goals.

- **Resilience**: Leadership often involves tackling challenges and setbacks head-on. A good leader is resilient and able to bounce back from adversity, learn from their experiences, and lead by example.

- **Decision-Making Skills**: Leaders sometimes need to make tough decisions. Having strong decision-making skills means being able to weigh options, consider different perspectives, and make informed choices.

- **Adaptability:** The more you adapt to changing circumstances, the easier it will be for you to climb the success ladder quickly. Things don't always go as planned, so being flexible and adaptable allows you to navigate challenges and seize opportunities.

- **Inspiration:** Great leaders inspire and motivate others to do their best. Whether through their words or actions, they encourage and uplift those around them.

- **Accountability:** Leaders always take responsibility for their actions and the outcomes of their decisions. They hold themselves and others accountable for their work and behavior.

Benefits of Leadership for Teens

Once you master this art of leading, it will help you in every sphere of life. From high school to college life and the workplace, your leadership skills will let you stand out and allow you to successfully take on responsibilities and delegate tasks effectively. It has multifaceted benefits for you:

Boost in Confidence: When you take on leadership roles, whether it is leading a school project or organizing a community event, you start believing in yourself more. You will see that you are capable of handling challenges and making a difference, which can really boost your confidence.

Learn to Speak Up: Being a leader means knowing what you want and being able to express it. Through leadership, you will learn to understand your own needs better and speak up for yourself. This skill is super important, not just now but also when you are dealing with teachers, bosses, or even your future colleagues.

Job Skills Galore: Believe it or not, the stuff you learn as a leader is exactly what employers are looking for. Things like teamwork, problem-solving, and managing your time well are all part of being a leader. So, by getting involved in leadership activities now, you are actually getting a head start on your future career!

Build Meaningful Relationships: As a leader, you will work closely with others, whether it is your peers, teachers, or community members. This gives you the chance to build great connections with others and build friendships that can last a lifetime. Plus, you will learn how to collaborate effectively with different types of people, which is a valuable skill in any area of life.

Learn from Failure: Not every leadership experience will go perfectly, and that is okay! In fact, it is through facing challenges and setbacks that you will grow the most. By leading projects or teams, you will learn how to bounce back from failure, adapt to new situations, and keep pushing forward. These are some basic skills that will serve you well in both your personal and professional life.

Make a Difference: Perhaps the most rewarding aspect of leadership is the opportunity to make a positive impact on others and your community. From organizing a charity fundraiser to mentoring younger students or advocating for important causes, your leadership efforts can truly change lives for the better. And there is no feeling quite like knowing you have made a difference in the world!

Ways you can develop leadership skills

"Can I really lead others? Do I have what it takes to feel empowered?" Yes! You do. While some people are naturally gifted leaders, leadership is still a skill that can be learned and developed over time as you grow. Since every individual is unique, we all need to work on our leadership skills at different levels. Some individuals might need to work a lot, while others would need just a little nudge to get going. However, the following simple ways can help you all discover your inner leadership potential and stand for what you believe in:

Take on responsibility: Responsibilities make you resilient and capable. Don't shy away from taking on different tasks, whether big or small.

Specify your long- and short-term goals: Set clear goals for yourself, both in the short-term and long-term. When you know what you want to achieve, it gives you direction and a sense of purpose, which helps you focus your efforts and make decisions that align with your objectives.

Explore Your Limits: Challenge yourself to try new things, take on new responsibilities, and push your boundaries a little every day.

Practice effective communication: Communication is key to leadership. Actively listen to others, articulate your ideas clearly, and learn to speak up confidently.

Develop emotional resilience: Employ all the emotional regulation techniques we have explored in the previous chapter to get hold of your feelings.

Accept uncertainty and change: In today's fast-paced world, change is inevitable. So, learn to accept uncertainty and adapt to new situations with resilience and flexibility.

Stay loyal to yourself and your principles: Stay true to your values, beliefs, and principles, even when faced with challenges or pressure to compromise.

Participate in extracurricular activities: Whether it is school sports teams, clubs, or volunteer groups, getting involved outside of the classroom in constructive and productive activities is a fantastic way to hone your leadership abilities.

Reach out to a Mentor: Look for mentors who can offer you guidance, support, and valuable insights based on their own experiences. A good mentor can give you great advice, honest feedback, and encouragement to learn and grow.

Be a Voice, Not an Echo: Never feel afraid to raise your voice and speak up to share your ideas, opinions, and perspectives in a polite and humble manner. Your unique voice and insights can put forth valuable contributions to discussions and decision-making processes in any situation.

Simply put:

"A leader is one who knows the way, goes the way, and shows the way."

And those profound words by John C. Maxwell bring us to the end of this chapter. Becoming a leader is not always about taking certain roles and positions in life; it is a journey that empowers you to the core. Once you adopt all the leadership skills like open communication, standing up for a cause, effective conflict resolution, and embracing your confidence, you inspire others as well. I believe that every kid is super talented and naturally born with leadership qualities; what they often lack is a little self-belief. To take concrete action and achieve your goals, you first need to convince yourself that you are very much capable and the world will follow suit. So, have some faith in your abilities, stand up for what you believe in, and make this world a better place.

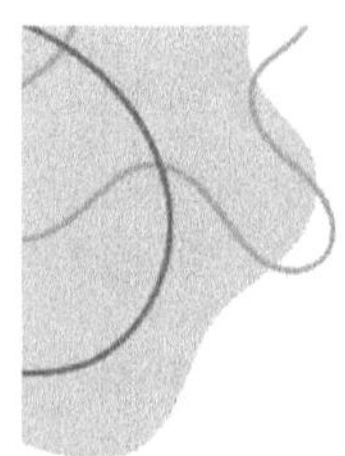

LEADING
FROM
WITHIN

- How effectively do I communicate my ideas and thoughts to others?

____

____

- Am I able to listen actively and empathetically to others' perspectives?

____

____

- How do I approach challenges or obstacles when working with a group?

____

____

- Am I able to identify solutions and make decisions in a timely manner?

____

____

- How do I make decisions when leading a group or team?

____

____

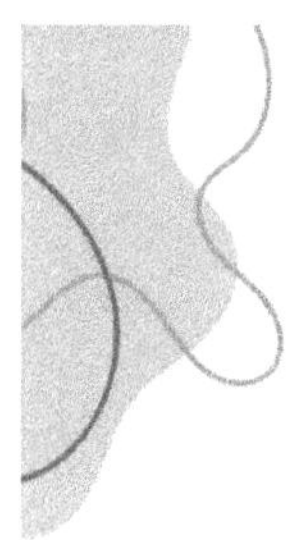

LEADING
FROM
WITHIN

- Do I take responsibility for my decisions and their outcomes?

  ____

  ____

- How do I handle conflicts or disagreements within a group?

  ____

  ____

- How do I inspire and motivate others to work towards a common goal?

  ____

  ____

- Am I able to delegate tasks effectively and empower others to take on leadership roles?

  ____

  ____

- Do I regularly evaluate progress and adjust plans as needed to stay on track?

  ____

  ____

Conclusion

With those reflective questions about leadership, we have reached the end of this book. I hope this comprehensive guide on life skills has been your go-to buddy on this crazy ride to adulthood. We have looked into some of the most essential life skills here, from the way to talk to people without freaking out to making tough decisions, managing time, organizing, bouncing back when life throws curveballs, cooking, and, most importantly, looking after yourself.

Each and every chapter has been packed with tips and tricks to help take control of your life in today's world and a few engaging activities. We started by learning the importance of all the essential skills that every teen needs to learn. Then, we delved deeper into each skill to explore the world full of learning opportunities. First, we looked into effective study methods and techniques to help you get on top of your academic game. With so many changes going around in life, it gets difficult to concentrate on your education and manage your grades. The tips and tricks shared in that chapter will help you utilize your study time in the most effective manner, and they will help you score well in all your upcoming tests and exams. Besides studies, another significant challenge of teen years is time management. That is why, in chapter three, we went through some of the most effective time-managing tricks that are even recommended by experts. When you manage your time well and keep all your things organized, your mind remains focused on the things that really matter. And that is how you climb the ladders of success in every realm of your life.

Right after understanding the importance of time management and organization, we deeply looked into the art of effective communication. From face-to-face communication skills to building strong and healthy relationships, we have explored some of the finest techniques to put your ideas and thoughts across. Then came the chapter about financial fitness. The purpose was to offer you detailed guidance about how to manage your money and put it to the right use without succumbing to the lure of impulse buying. Later in the book, we discussed the power of effective choices, methods to ensure online safety, self-care practices, basic hygiene habits, and techniques to unlock your inner leadership potential. Perhaps there was so much more than I can mention here. The aim was simple, to provide you with valuable knowledge and practical tips to help you become the best version of yourself.

And guess what? You are more capable than you give yourself credit for. Every bump in the road that you ever faced was just a chance for you to level up. What matters the most is that you keep striving, evolving, and growing to become the better version of yourself. Even finishing this book is a testament to the efforts you are putting into learning something new and powerful. And you really deserve a pat on the back for mustering up the courage to acknowledge your inadequacies and work on them. By polishing up those life skills, you are basically arming yourself with superpowers to tackle whatever life throws your way, chase those dreams, and live a life with peace of heart and ultimate success.

Now that you are armed with knowledge, it is time to put these skills to work. Grab every chance to learn, grow, and make a mark on the world. Believe in yourself, stick to what you stand for, and don't sleep on the impact you can have on others. While heading into the next chapter of your life, don't forget you are not flying solo. Lean on your squad, your family, and anyone who has your back and believes in you.

So, go out there with your head held high, ready to take on anything with guts, smarts, and a whole lot of heart. Celebrate your victories along the way and learn from your mistakes without letting them stop you. And never stop hustling to be this amazing version of yourself. The world is counting on you to shine bright. Go ahead and light up the sky!

Your Opinion Matters!

hope this book has been a total game-changer for you! Now, it is your turn to step up and make it happen. Try out the tips and techniques you have learned and see how they can make your life even better. Don't keep it all to yourself; share what you have discovered with your friends to support each other through this dynamic digital world.

Your feedback is invaluable, and I would love to hear from you! Please leave a review and let me know what worked and what could be better. Together, we can create a brighter and stronger future and make this journey to adulthood uniquely fulfilling!

About the Author

S. Connor has dedicated over two decades of professional service to the corporate world, providing invaluable support to top management at a leading multinational corporation. Throughout her career, she has demonstrated remarkable perseverance, determination, and an unwavering commitment to excellence.

Beyond her professional accomplishments, she excels in various domains, such as sports and drawing, and has received multiple awards. Yet, her most cherished role is that of a devoted mother to two wonderful children. With its joys and challenges, parenthood is a source of inspiration that fuels her creativity and empathy.

Having witnessed the complexities of life and watched her children navigate adolescence, S. Connor profoundly understands the challenges that today's young adults face. Her refined communication skills, developed during her successful corporate career, allow her to translate intricate ideas into relatable messages within her books. Whether addressing mental health issues or providing teenagers with the tools to navigate adolescence confidently, her goal is to inspire and foster a deeper understanding of life's diverse aspects.

S. Connor is determined to use her writing skills to inspire change and promote personal growth and fulfillment among young adults and individuals.

Acknowledgements

Firstly, I would like to thank the Almighty God, our creator, Jehovah, for showering abundant blessings on me and for giving me the ability and insight to write this book.

I want to sincerely thank my loving family for always supporting and cheering me up as I wrote this book - and a special thank you to my loving husband, Adrian Connor, who always stood by me and believed in me. I am grateful to my children, Steffi and Andrew, for their patience and understanding throughout this journey. They inspire me in everything that I do.

I am also grateful to my very caring parents and in-laws, who have never stopped showing me their unconditional love.

To all my friends, thank you for being there for me. Finally, thank you to my mentor. His guidance and motivation made this writing and publication possible.

References

8 Simple Steps to Good Decision-Making for Teens by Ivana Pejakovic | Noomii. (n.d.). https://www.noomii.com/articles/809-8-simple-steps-to-good-decisionmaking-for-teens

16 Must-Have leadership qualities. (n.d.). https://www.ollusa.edu/blog/leadership-qualities.html

A leader is one who knows the way, goes the way, and shows the way. (John C. Maxwell) — Steemit. (n.d.). Steemit. https://steemit.com/leadership/@alwaysgrateful/a-leader-is-one-who-knows-the-way-goes-the-way-and-shows-the-way-john-c-maxwell

Academy, C. (2023, September 28). 5 Secrets of Smart Students: Effective study Tips for High School. https://www.connectionsacademy.com/support/resources/article/4-steps-to-forming-effective-study-skills-in-high-school/

Ackerman, C. E., MA. (2024, March 4). Cognitive restructuring techniques for reframing thoughts. PositivePsychology.com. https://positivepsychology.com/cbt-cognitive-restructuring-cognitive-distortions/

ActiveCollab. (2024, May 13). ParEto principle for time management and prioritization. ActiveCollab. https://activecollab.com/blog/project-management/pareto-principle#:~:text=In%20time%20management%2C%2080%25%20of,20%25%20of%20the%20pea%20pods

Adele says she started working out to address panic attacks after her divorce. (2024, May 14). TODAY.com. https://www.today.com/health/health/adele-weight-loss-rcna150970

Adesakin, S. (2022, September 15). Save money, and money will save you - Businessday NG. Businessday NG. https://businessday.ng/interview/women-in-business/article/save-money-and-money-will-save-you/#:~:text=A%20Jamaican%20proverb%20says%2C%20%E2%80%9CSave,and%20money%20will%20save%20you.%E2%80%9D

Admin. (2019, May 25). A Journey of a Thousand Miles Begins with a Single Step - Meaning - Literary Devices. Literary Devices. https://literarydevices.net/a-journey-of-a-thousand-miles-begins-with-a-single-step/

Administrator. (2020, February 25). Storing fresh fruits and veggies; freezing fruits and veggies - double up food bucks. Double up Food Bucks. https://doubleupcolorado.org/storing-fresh-fruits-and-veggies-freezing-fruits-and-veggies/#:~:text=Most%20produce%20maintains%20its%20quality,texture%2C%20and%20nutrients%20during%20freezing

Ali. (2020, March 29). No-Bake energy bites. Gimme Some Oven. https://www.gimmesomeoven.com/no-bake-energy-bites/

Bieber, C. (n.d.). This simple rule has reduced my impulse purchases. The Motley Fool. https://www.fool.com/the-ascent/personal-finance/articles/this-simple-rule-has-reduced-my-impulse-purchases/

Britannica money. (n.d.). https://www.britannica.com/money/what-is-the-50-30-20-rule#:~:text=The%20rule%20targets%2050%25%20of,or%20adding%20to%20your%20savings

Can I Wear the Same Pad All Day? (n.d.). Kids Health.org. https://kidshealth.org/en/teens/changing-pads.html

Children. (2024, March 18). Linus Pauling Institute. https://lpi.oregonstate.edu/mic/life-stages/children

Clear, J. (2020, February 4). The Ivy Lee Method: the daily routine for peak productivity. James Clear. https://jamesclear.com/ivy-lee

Coping Skills for Teens - Modern Recovery Services. (n.d.). Modern Recovery Services. https://modernrecoveryservices.com/wellness/coping/life-stages/children-and-teens/

Cyberbullying: What is it and how to stop it. (n.d.). UNICEF. https://www.unicef.org/end-violence/how-to-stop-cyberbullying

Diet: a balanced diet and your health | Guides | HIV i-Base. (n.d.). https://i-base.info/guides/side/diet-a-balanced-diet-and-your-health

Dwyer, F. M., & Moore, D. M. (n.d.). Effect of color coding on cognitive style. https://eric.ed.gov/?id=ED347986

"Education is the passport to the future, for tomorrow belongs to those who prepare for it today." — Lifting As We Climb Consulting. (n.d.). https://www.liftingasweclimbconsulting.com/testimonials/education-is-the-passport-to-the-future-for-tomorrow-belongs-to-those-who-prepare-for-it-today/

FDA error. (n.d.). FDA. https://www.fda.gov/consumers/consumer-updates/facts-tampons-and-how-use-them-safely#:~:text=Tampons%20are%20not%20intended%20to,the%20lowest%20absorbency%20tampon%20needed.

Food Freezing Guide. (2024, January 9). NDSU Agriculture. https://www.ndsu.edu/agriculture/extension/publications/food-freezing-guide

Food poisoning: How long can you safely keep leftovers? (2024, May 14). Mayo Clinic. https://www.mayoclinic.org/healthy-lifestyle/nutrition-and-healthy-eating/expert-answers/food-safety/faq-

20058500#:~:text=Leftovers%20can%20be%20kept%20for,safe%20for%20a%20long%20time.

Fowler, P. (2024, March 5). Breathing techniques for stress relief. WebMD. https://www.webmd.com/balance/stress-management/stress-relief-breathing-techniques

Generic, Y. T. (2024, February 22). How To Help Teenagers Make Good Decisions | Spark their Future. Spark Their Future. https://www.sparktheirfuture.qld.edu.au/how-to-help-your-teen-make-good-decisions-about-school-and-life/

Harvard Health. (2024, April 3). Understanding the stress response. https://www.health.harvard.edu/staying-healthy/understanding-the-stress-response

Hope, A. (2023, December 7). Effective study skills: Encouraging good teen study habits | Boo Roo and Tigger too. Boo Roo and Tigger Too. https://www.boorooandtiggertoo.com/effective-study-skills/

How can you use the Eisenhower matrix for effective studying? (2023, December 16). www.linkedin.com. https://www.linkedin.com/advice/3/how-can-you-use-eisenhower-matrix-effective-j0fgf#:~:text=The%20Eisenhower%20matrix%20is%20a,is%20named%20after%20Dwight%20D

How to use the 2-Minute Rule for More Productivity and Less Procrastination. (n.d.). https://www.usemotion.com/blog/2-minute-rule#:~:text=The%20two%2Dminute%20rule%20is,to%20your%20to%2Ddo%20list

Hugh Jackman Quote: "Now I meditate twice a day for half an hour. In meditation, I can let go of everything. I'm not Hugh Jackman. I'm not a . . ." (n.d.). https://quotefancy.com/quote/1252303/Hugh-Jackman-Now-I-meditate-twice-a-day-for-half-an-hour-In-meditation-I-can-let-go-of

Hussein, Z. M., Dehham, S. H., & Hasan, A. a. N. (2019). The impact of using chunking technique on developing reading skill and perception of intermediate school students. Indian Journal of Public Health Research and Development, 10(6), 1186. https://doi.org/10.5958/0976-5506.2019.01452.9

Inspirational Quote by John Powell. (n.d.). Criteria for Success. https://criteriaforsuccess.com/inspirational-quote-by-john-powell/

Internet safety for teens 101 – Your comprehensive guide. (2023, August 18). Acronis. https://www.acronis.com/en-us/blog/posts/internet-safety-for-teens/#:~:text=Avoid%20suspicious%20websites%20and%20downloads,that%20can%20compromise%20their%20devices.&text=Recognize%20and%20avoid%20phishing%20scams,them%20aware%20of%20phishing%20attacks

Journaling for Emotional Wellness - Health Encyclopedia - University of Rochester Medical Center. (n.d.). https://www.urmc.rochester.edu/encyclopedia/content.aspx?ContentID=4552&ContentTypeID=1

Man's Search for Meaning by Viktor Frankl: Summary & Notes. (2023, November 18). Calvin Rosser. https://calvinrosser.com/notes/mans-search-for-meaning-viktor-frankl/

Marianne Williamson Quote: "Every decision you make reflects your evaluation of who you are." (n.d.). https://quotefancy.com/quote/860721/Marianne-Williamson-Every-decision-you-make-reflects-your-evaluation-of-who-you-are

McCaffery, S. (2024, May 29). Feel the fear and Do it Anyway By Susan Jeffers, Ph.D. Books You Gotta Read. https://booksyougottaread.com/2023/04/06/feel-the-fear-do-it-anyway-by-susan-jeffers-ph-d/

McNamara, B. (2019, April 17). Sophie Turner opened up about therapy and mental health medication. Teen Vogue.

https://www.teenvogue.com/story/sophie-turner-opened-up-about-therapy-and-mental-health-medication

Merton, S. (2023, July 24). 'Slow and Steady Wins the Race': Definition, Meaning, and Examples. Writing Tips. https://writingtips.org/slow-and-steady-wins-the-race/#:~:text=%E2%80%98Slow%20and%20steady%20wins%20the%20race%E2%80%99%20is%20a,will%20allow%20you%20to%20conquer%20any%20problem%20eventually.

MindTools | Home. (n.d.). https://www.mindtools.com/aef000n/cognitive-restructuring

Motivation, U. (2021, June 25). "You will either learn to manage money, or the lack of it will manage you." -Dave Ramsey - Undefeated Motivation. Undefeated Motivation. https://undefeatedmotivation.com/quotes/you-will-either-learn-to-manage-money-or-the-lack-of-it-will-manage-you-dave-ramsey-quote/

MSEd, K. C. (2022, December 19). How chunking pieces of information can improve Memory. Verywell Mind. https://www.verywellmind.com/chunking-how-can-this-technique-improve-your-memory-2794969

MSEd, K. C. (2024, May 14). What to know about Mindfulness Meditation. Verywell Mind. https://www.verywellmind.com/mindfulness-meditation-88369

Naftulin, J. (2023, January 19). 15 celebrities with anxiety who have spoken out. Health. https://www.health.com/condition/anxiety/celeb-struggle-anxiety

Nagi, & Nagi. (2023, July 30). My best grilled cheese sandwich. RecipeTin Eats. https://www.recipetineats.com/grilled-cheese-sandwich/

Novak, M. C. (2020, March 2). Time Batching: The Ultimate guide to boost productivity. GoSkills.com. https://www.goskills.com/Office-Productivity/Resources/Time-batching

"Only handle it once" — How to use the Ohio method. (2024, May 17). Niels Bohrmann. https://nielsbohrmann.com/only-handle-it-once/#:~:text=The%20OHIO%20method%20(%E2%80%9COnly%20Handle%20It%20Once%E2%80%9D)%20is,The%20classic%20example%20is%20email

Park, R. (2024, May 9). How to Use "I" Statements: A Clear Guide. https://www.firstsession.com/resources/how-to-use-i-statements#:~:text=%22I%22%20statements%20focus%20on%20the,avoid%20attacking%20or%20blaming%20others

Patwal, S. (2023, August 18). Personal hygiene for teens: importance and tips to teach them. MomJunction. https://www.momjunction.com/articles/hygiene-tips-for-your-teens_00116170/

Pierce, R. (2023, October 18). 13 Practical time management skills to teach teens | Life Skills Advocate. Life Skills Advocate. https://lifeskillsadvocate.com/blog/13-practical-time-management-skills-to-teach-teens/

Pomodoro® Technique - Time Management Method. (n.d.). https://www.pomodorotechnique.com/

Progressive muscle relaxation. (n.d.). https://www.utoledo.edu/studentaffairs/counseling/anxietytoolbox/pmr.html#:~:text=PMR%20is%20an%20exercise%20that,same%20time%20experience%20anxiety%20symptoms.

Quality is a habit! (n.d.). https://opentrainingcollege.com/quality-is-a-habit-managing-service-quality/

Quoatable. (2023, February 3). Kin Hubbard Quote: The safe way to double your money is to fold it over once and put it in your pocket. Quoatable. https://www.quoatable.com/kin-hubbard-quote-the-safe-way-to-double-your-money-is-to-fold-it-over-once-and-put-it-in-your-pocket/

Rd, J. K. M. (2022, June 20). Healthy Eating for Teens: A complete guide. Healthline. https://www.healthline.com/nutrition/healthy-eating-for-teens#nutrient-needs

Rearick, L. (2018, February 9). Zendaya colors to cope with stress. Teen Vogue. https://www.teenvogue.com/story/zendaya-coloring-stress

Safinabakes. (2023, April 20). Easy microwave chocolate mug cake. Allrecipes. https://www.allrecipes.com/recipe/241038/microwave-chocolate-mug-cake/

Schwahn, L., & Ayoola, E. (2024, February 22). What is the 'Cash stuffing' envelope system? NerdWallet. https://www.nerdwallet.com/article/finance/envelope-system#:~:text=The%20concept%20is%20simple%3A%20Take,using%20actual%20cash%20and%20envelopes

Simplilearn. (2024, April 21). Top 16 time management skills to help you become a success. Simplilearn.com. https://www.simplilearn.com/time-management-skills-article

Stacy, E. M., & Cain, J. (2015). Note-taking and handouts in the digital age. American Journal of Pharmaceutical Education, 79(7), 107. https://doi.org/10.5688/ajpe797107

Tania. (2022, May 24). Mixed Berry Smoothie with Yogurt. Cooking for My Soul. https://cookingformysoul.com/mixed-berry-yogurt-smoothie/

Tbrg. (2022, March 24). 10 ways you can develop leadership skills as a teen. The Big Red Group. https://www.thebigredgroup.com/10-ways-you-can-develop-leadership-skills-as-a-teen/

The Digital Wellness Lab. (2024, January 12). Family Guide to teaching kids and teens essential digital skills. https://digitalwellnesslab.org/family-guides/empowering-digital-natives-a-guide-to-teaching-kids-and-teens-essential-digital-skills/

The influence of chunking on reading comprehension: Investigating the Acquisition of Chunking Skill. (2013). The Journal of Asia TEFL, Vol.10(No. 4), 163–183. https://www.asiatefl.org/main/download_pdf.php?i=38&c=1391762169&fn=10_4_06.pdf

Thrive Training and Consulting. (2021, November 11). Tips for teens: Building healthy communication skills - Thrive Training Consulting. Thrive Training Consulting. https://www.thrivetrainingconsulting.com/tips-for-teens-building-healthy-communication-skills/

Time management. (n.d.). https://www.ou.edu/ucc/resources/time-management

United States Institute of Peace. (n.d.). What is Active Listening? https://www.usip.org/public-education-new/what-active-listening

Visions. (2022, October 31). 12 Ways to practice self care for Teens. Visions Treatment Centers. https://visionsteen.com/12-ways-to-practice-self-care-for-teens/

Western & Southern Financial Group. (2023, October 18). Money Management for Teens: Important lessons to teach your kids. https://www.westernsouthern.com/personal-finance/money-management-for-teens

What is Budgeting Software? (n.d.). https://www.oracle.com/pk/performance-management/planning/zero-based-budgeting/#:~:text=Zero%2Dbased%20budgeting%20(ZBB),and%20adjusting%20it%20as%20needed